HEAVEN ON EARTH

JIM GRASSI

HARVEST HOUSE PUBLISHERS
Eugene, Oregon 97402

Cover by Garborg Design Works, Minneapolis, Minnesota

Cover art: Valley of Peace
© 1997 Thomas Kinkade, Media Arts Group, Inc., San Jose, CA.
For more information regarding Thomas Kinkade, please call 1-800-366-3733.

HEAVEN ON EARTH

Copyright © 1997 by Jim Grassi
Published by Harvest House Publishers
Eugene, Oregon 97402

Library of Congress Cataloging-in-Publication Data

Grassi, James E., 1943–
   Heaven on earch / Jim Grassi.
     p. cm.
   Includes bibliographical references (p.).
   ISBN 1-56507-635-4
   1. Men—Religious life.   2. Fishing—Religious aspects—Christianity.
3. Fishing—Anecdotes.   4. Fishers—Religious life.
I. Title.
BV4528.2G73   1997
248.8'42—dc21   97-1218
                                              CIP

Printed in the United States of America.

97   98   99   00   01   02   03   / BP /   10   9   8   7   6   5   4   3   2   1

To Louise, my devoted wife,
who keeps me standing in the center of the boat.
Thank you for all your
unconditional love and support.

Contents

ACKNOWLEDGMENTS

As executive director of a thriving ministry, my creel is filled with enough new projects and programs that I generally don't need to think for a minute about whether I should take on any new tasks. However, when I finished my first book, *Promising Waters,* I had no way of knowing that within four weeks it would hit the bestseller list. It was then that Harvest House Publishers asked me to develop a complementary work.

Before agreeing to this task, I confided in a few close friends and spoke to my heavenly Father about the project. I knew it would stretch my stamina and skills to the limit. After a time of contemplation, I decided to go forward with the project.

Throughout the writing of this book, I've enjoyed a tremendous sense of peace and protection. Not only that, I found that God taught me numerous lessons during the 15-hour days that were often required to accomplish this work while at the same time shepherding our ministry. I give all the honor, praise, and glory to God, who through His divine grace and mercy allowed me to finish on schedule. *Thank you Jesus!*

As is true in accomplishing any substantial task, there is a host of behind-the-scenes individuals that provided tangible support and assistance during this project. It's much the same with fishing. As we read in Luke 5, Jesus showed His disciples that fishing (like ministry) is a team effort. It requires those willing to mend nets, row boats, sort fish, repair fishing tackle, and pull on lines, all so the master fisherman can cast his net and catch the fish.

Those who said "Go for it Jim" were the ones who came beside me and lifted an oar, mended a net, or helped provide resources that would allow me the necessary time to research and write this book. Thank you J.D. and Linda Larson, Rick Haley, Dr. and Suzanne Downs, Jeff Klippenes, Jon Adams, Pastor Jon McNeff, Anne Marie Taylor, Jim and Bobbie Knuppe, the PTLA Corporation, my board of directors, the LGFP Proteam, and LGFM volunteers. Whatever "catch" comes from this book is due in part to your unselfish and supportive hearts.

I want to thank the wonderfully supportive staff and editors with Harvest House Publishers. I especially thank Ron Rhodes for his expertise and continual guidance.

Finally, a special thanks to my fishing buddy and artist extraordinaire, Thomas Kinkade, for permission to use "The Valley of Peace" as the cover illustration for this book. His work graces and embraces the concept of *Heaven on Earth.*

Introduction

Tucked in the annals of fishing are stories of numerous great anglers (or fishermen). Many have mastered the sport, and several have become nationally recognized for their accomplishments. But precious few have demonstrated the Christian character that qualifies them to be identified as "champions of the faith."

Heaven on Earth is an adventure book about life and living. It opens the thoughts and hearts of prominent men who have unique and exciting stories to share about fishing and faith. These men *are* champions of the faith.

Each of their adventure stories profiles a trait or quality that distinguishes that person's character. I trust that the humorous anecdotes and entertaining parables will keep things lively and stimulating.

As I ponder the use of parables as a teaching tool, it strikes me that Jesus did not come as a religious leader in any traditional sense. He took His ministry to the city streets of Galilee, to homes and fields, and wherever else the common people might be found. He taught people through metaphors, beatitudes, proverbs, and dialogue. His most distinctive method of teaching, however, was His use of parables. Moral truths and ideals were communicated through simple comparisons or examples drawn from everyday experiences. Following Jesus' lead, I hope to communicate lessons about faith drawn from their everyday fishing stories of fifteen great leaders.

These godly men just happen to enjoy the sport of fishing as much as I do. They are "real guys" who have faced many challenges and struggles in life, but who faithfully continue to trust in God. They have a consistent Christian experience and are considered national role models in their respective fields. They represent a variety of backgrounds—including a professional athlete, television personality, artist, business executive, pastor, musician, psychologist, and an outdoor writer. Despite their diverse interests, however, all would consider God's great outdoors as their preferred environment.

It is my hope that the following stories and anecdotes will come to life in your spirit as you witness the interplay of faith and fishing in these men's lives. And may it please the Lord to help you grow in commitment and character while experiencing these "stories with a promise"!

Hank Parker

Jim Grassi with Jimmy Houston

Jim Grassi with Thomas Kinkade

Homer Circle

Al Lindner with son Troy

1

First Cast

Jim Grassi

Fishing continues to be one of the most popular sports. Men, women, boys, girls, disabled persons, presidents, and common laborers have joined the ranks of folks pursuing the denizens of the deep.

Today more than 70 million people claim fishing as their favorite pastime in the United States and Canada. One-third of all anglers are women. (An "angler" is someone who fishes with a hook.) Presently over $69.4 billion per year are spent on this exciting sport.

Fishing is one of the few activities that can embrace the entire family while encouraging communication and teamwork. I believe God intended people to fully participate in this diversion. Why else would He have made the earth with three-quarters of its surface area filled with water and fish?

I can think of at least six reasons why people fish:

1. *Fishing Is Fun*. Fishing brims with adventure and exploration. It allows people to frolic in the sun while challenging a relatively small creature that can cause grown men and women of great refinement to yell, squeal, laugh, shout, and otherwise become hysterical. Where else could a scholarly young lad with a slight build be able to compete with a

world-class athlete and know he has an equal chance of catching the biggest fish in the pond? The mysteries and elusive nature surrounding the sport create lifelong amusement that tantalizes the mind and soul.

For some, fishing is "the art of casting, trolling, jigging, or spinning while freezing, sweating, drooling, swatting, or swearing." It is easy for a serious fisherman to become overwhelmed with the thought, "So many lures . . . so little time."

I believe we should make every effort to keep fishing a fun activity, especially for kids. We need to make it entertaining. Pick a good weather day during a time when the bite is hot, even if it's just bluegill (brim) fishin'. Put one line in the water with live bait and let the kids cast another rod using a lure. *And be prepared for some fun.*

The development of casting skills is enjoyable to most people—including kids. You can be the encourager and netter until the little ones catch all they want. Then on the way home you can drive by their favorite fast-food restaurant and buy them a burger and shake. Just before they fall off to sleep, relive the adventure with them and share your genuine excitement. They will remember you and that day for the rest of their lives. Now *that* is fun!

Don't put so much emphasis on the catch. *Honor the experience.* Remember—if you caught fish every time you went fishin', it wouldn't be called fishin', it would be called catchin'.

One more thing. An important key to being a successful angler is to remember that the best days to go fishing are on those that end in "y."

2. *Fishing Provides Food.* Ever since the time of Adam and Eve, human beings have realized the importance of fish to their diet. It is low in fat and high in protein and vitamin E. There are many examples in Scripture of fish being eaten as part of a meal. For many cultures, eating fish is the only tangible means of survival. Personally, I release about 99 percent of the fish I catch, only to go down to the local grocery store

to buy commercially harvested fish for dinner. Unfortunately, most of the waters I boat on do not have enough fish to accommodate the ever-increasing number of anglers.

3. *Fishing Is an Escape.* The stresses of a hurried world creep in on all of us. We need continual opportunities to retreat and rest. Scripture is filled with examples of people who found their way to the shoreline of a lake, stream, or ocean to relax and reflect. Fishing was such an important part of Bible-time culture, I'm sure that many folks grabbed their willow stick rods and hooks with some bait while they contemplated God's plan for their lives. For me, fishing is the best medicine I can take. I often experience those difficult problems of life trickling down my line into the vast sea of tranquillity. It is a great time to listen to God while reflecting on His blessings and His beautiful creation.

4. *Fishing Is a Challenge.* Few sports offer the diverse challenge that is presented in fishing. Whether you enjoy stalking a weary brown trout in crystal clear water or challenging a 1,000-pound blue marlin with standup fighting gear, it's all formidable. On a professional level, there are those who have made more than a million dollars competing against other highly skilled anglers. For some, though, the rigors of competition can be so intense that they lose sight of the fun.

For beginners and youngsters, fishing is an opportunity to pit their increasing skills against squirming-wiggling packages of joy who wish they hadn't made the mistake of biting that hook. A young child at one of our Let's Go Fishing Ministries shared with me his fishing philosophy: "Once the bait hits the water and sinks to the bottom, it's up to God as to which hook the fish is going to pick and choose."

5. *Fishing Brings Companionship.* I can think of no better way to spend a day than fishing out of my bass boat with a relative or friend. As part of my ministry, I generally try to provide some counseling and guidance along the way. I try to get people out on the boat because I know how the experience of fishing can relax them and help stimulate communication.

6. *It's Heaven on Earth*. Heaven is somewhat of a mystery. But glimpses of heaven that we see through Christ's teachings and the book of Revelation suggest that we will be absolutely delighted with all that encompasses this wonderful place. Perhaps the closest we can get to heaven on earth is to experience the wonder and peace that comes when one ventures out to a pristine stream where nature's magnificence is on full display. That's why I've titled this book, "Heaven on Earth."

Time Well Spent

I've *never* considered a day wasted if I spent it fishing. As the bumper sticker reads, "The worst day fishing is better than the best day working."

Despite the aforementioned benefits, though, there are some who believe that fishing is not very productive. Our society tends to value time as related to success and accomplishments.

Fishing is not always "productive" in the sense that one may not always have a tangible product (a stringer of fish) at the end of the day. Still, the intangible benefits make it all worthwhile. Herbert Hoover was an avid angler and passed on this message to all who might consider the sport:

> Tis the chance to wash one's soul with pure air, with the rush of the brook, or with the shimmer of the sun on the blue water. It brings meekness and inspiration from the decency of nature, charity toward tackle makers, patience toward fish, a mockery of profits and egos, a quieting of hate, a rejoicing that you do not have to decide a darned thing until next week. And it is discipline in the equality of men, for all men are equal before fish.

The First Century Fishermen-Disciples

In researching and writing my first book, *Promising Waters—Stories of Fishing and Following Jesus,* I was struck with the numerous parallels and correlations that exist between the disciplines of fishing and discipleship. I believe it was no coincidence that Jesus picked eight fishermen to be among His 12 disciples (John 21). These simple Galilean fishermen were rough and somewhat pedestrian in their thinking. Their Jewish roots, filled with passion and prejudice, often presented challenges to learning new ideas. Despite their obvious skill and success in the fishing community, these practical, hardworking men would soon give up their musty nets and smelly fish to catch the vision of Christ's ministry. Jesus said to them, "Come, follow me, and I will make you fishers of men" (Matthew 4:19).

Why did our Savior relate so well to fishermen? And how are the attributes of fishermen transferable to discipling others?

Fishermen are a unique breed and are rarely understood by others. More often than not, they are considered a little odd or eccentric. Likewise, fishers of men don't generally lend themselves toward a neat ecclesiastical job description.

Fishermen are inquisitive people of adventure and exploration. A disciple is never content with the routine and the mundane.

Fishermen keep focused on what they are doing. A disciple fixes his eyes on Jesus, and as he walks in the power of the Holy Spirit he tackles each challenge and embraces each relationship as an opportunity to serve our Lord.

Fishermen have faith that every cast will produce a fish. They believe that just *one more cast* will be the one that yields a fish. Fishers of men live by faith, not by sight (2 Corinthians 5:7). This is the same faith Peter demonstrated when he cast his bare hook into the Sea of Galilee and caught a fish with a coin in its mouth (Matthew 17:27).

Fishermen are passionate and persistent. They spend countless hours preparing, analyzing, evaluating, and pursuing their beloved sport. They challenge the fish and don't give up. Similarly, a disciple attacks his mission with dedication and zeal.

Fishermen are people of skill and knowledge. They study the habits and habitats of fish while routinely practicing their casting skills. Likewise, fishers of men understand the sin-filled environment in which they live and work, while carefully devoting themselves to preparatory prayer and study.

Fishermen are eager to share their knowledge, experiences, and skill with others. Disciples are equally interested in sharing the joy of our Lord and Savior with others.

Fishermen take risks and overcome the obstacles before them. Often the more difficult challenge provides a bigger and better reward. The disciple is no different. We must be willing to risk by "fishing deeper waters" for the bountiful harvest God has prepared (Luke 5).

Fishermen catch fish. True disciples don't just fill a pew on Sunday; they're actively involved in "catching" others for Christ (Matthew 4:19).

As we consider how fishing relates to discipleship, it is clear that Jesus wanted to relate to men who understood the challenges of life in a unique way, men who dealt with the mysteries of nature. He realized that many of the principles, methods, and techniques used in relating to people on a spiritual basis are very similar to those used in fishing. By showing the disciples how to apply His teachings, they could then pursue the ultimate fishing challenge—becoming *fishers of men*. Jesus wanted to lead them on the fishing adventure of a lifetime where the rewards have eternal consequences with net-breaking excitement.

"I Fish—Therefore I Am!"

I believe it's important for a fisherman—whether of fish *or* men—to be a philosopher. I first realized this when I attended a fly-fishing club meeting. I noticed how many guys stood around in their Eddie Bauer garb looking upward as if the Rapture were about to happen. As I entered into dialogue with these sages, it soon became apparent that it was more important to have a philosophy of fishing than to have fished all the local streams.

While reading some of the wonderful works of Patrick F. McManus (a modern-day Tom Sawyer), I realized where and how my philosophy developed. I agree with McManus that fishing turns people into philosophers. When I was about five years old, I caught my first fish. The fishing bug really bit me, and by my teen years I had collected enough equipment to outfit two sporting goods stores.

We didn't live very close to good fishing areas, so much of my time was spent sitting on my bed (a make-believe boat) and casting into the closet. My mom didn't understand my preoccupation until one day I said something like, "I fish—therefore I am." She walked off muttering something about how Elvis and rock 'n roll had messed up my mind.

When I registered for college, I entered as a pre-theology major, which, of course, was part of the philosophy department. After pondering my future as a fisherman-philosopher-theologian, I began to collect a number of thoughts that made some sense to me. With further inspiration from the writings of philosophers like McManus and Homer Circle, I continued to amaze others with my reflective thinking. Through our Let's Go Fishing Ministry we developed a "Fishing Club of Volunteers" who ascribe to the following deep thoughts:

- The worse the fisherman, the better the philosopher.

- Fishing is always better yesterday.

- So many flies . . . so little time.

- How much does a fish weigh? It depends on who caught it!

- You'll always catch your biggest fish the day you left your net and camera at home.

- The greatest rate of growth for a fish is between the time you catch it and the time you first tell your friends about it.

- Your tackle box will always open and spill just after you've organized it.

- Smoked carp tastes just as good as smoked salmon when you ain't got smoked salmon.

- The two best times to fish are when it's raining and when it's not.

- I fish—therefore I lie.

- Anytime a man ain't fishin', he is frittering away his time.

- Hittin' all the holes, reelin' in all the souls.

- Our mission—soul fishin'.

Reel Fishermen—Real Disciples

Most of us develop our passion for fishing at a young age. Some develop a passion in later years. But all "reel fishermen" have an ambition to catch fish.

Similarly, many people who receive Jesus Christ as Savior do so prior to 18 years of age. How about you? Have you taken the opportunity to consider your eternal destiny?

Jesus elected to use common fishermen to be among a small group of men that would change the world. These ordinary men were trained and educated by our Lord to utilize their individual spiritual gifts to help populate a heavenly kingdom.

Comparably, when we accept the precious gift of Jesus Christ and bring a truly repentant heart to God's throne, we are promised spiritual gifts that can be used for His glory. We must be willing to use those gifts and offer them to God so that He can multiply what we have. If we are truly committed to His cause, there is no telling what He can do with our "small loaves and fishes" (*see* John 6:1-14). Perhaps the simple prayer of Dottie Lovelady best encapsulates the thankful heart of one who has experienced just what God can do through a committed life:

> Father I thank you that you have accepted my offering of myself! Even though I have had little to give, you have taken that and multiplied it to do much more than I ever expected. Somehow, I feel like the boy with five loaves and two fishes.

I pray that the stories of fishing and faith expressed in this book will encourage you in your spiritual growth. In fact, my heart's desire is that *all* my ministry would be an encouragement to those who are not yet disciples; a guide and challenge to those who consider themselves followers of Christ; and a source of biblical principles that fishermen can utilize in catching both fish *and* men.

This book is brimming with anecdotes, biblical stories, angling experiences, humor, and real life challenges. It is intended to help you discover unique insights from God's Word that will help you better understand yourself, others, and God's character.

Are you ready to sharpen those hooks, string up the rods, and fill your boat with gas? It's time to blast off and seek out those unique "Fishing Adventures—Stories with a Promise." *Let's go fishing!*

Personal Growth

- What personal traits and qualities do you most identify with?

- Where are you in your spiritual journey? Are you willing to explore your faith and look at the possibilities of how God might use you to encourage others?

- You can't catch a fish if you don't go to the lake, stream, pond, or ocean. Are you willing to leave the comforts of home (your church) to explore the sea of life (the world around you) where fish are hungry for the offerings you can provide?

2

The Christian Disciple

Fishing with Jay Carty

What does a six-foot-eight-inch former professional basketball player know about fishing? I'm not sure even Jay Carty would identify himself as an avid angler. He certainly enjoys the sport and has identified some of the more fascinating aspects of such species as carp, trout, and bass. But more importantly, Jay has caught the vision of being a "fisher of men," and he does it very well.

In 1970 Jay's book *Something's Fishy* was published. As a gifted storyteller and humorist, Jay developed a unique correlation between certain types of fish and our commitment to be followers of Jesus. To help understand Jay's wit, I've embellished a few of his definitions:

Carp—(1) A trash fish. Carp are bottom-feeders. As they cruise the murky waters, their ugly lips turn down-ward and play vacuum cleaner, sucking up all the junk they can find. They're scavengers and scum suckers. They especially enjoy fish eggs. Like rats, carp are prolific breeders. (2) People who feed on the debase and immoral things of the world. (3) Sin that renders a believer powerless, which subsequently keeps a nonbeliever from believing.

Bass—(1) A game fish that is weary and protective. Bass carefully guard their territory and keep a vigilant eye on every aspect of their environment. They seem to have passion, a disposition that creates excitement and zeal for life. They are alert and very selective feeders. (2) A sold-out, on-fire, goin'-for-it, Jesus-lovin' believer. A true disciple.

Trout—(1) A game fish that sometimes acts like a bass. Trout are not as protective about their nests and will readily eat their young. They sometimes hang out with other species, thereby confusing anglers looking at electronic fish locators who are trying to determine what type of fish they have under their boat. In a stream they can be found right next to trash fish like suckers, carp, or squawfish. (2) A luke-warm Christian. A person trying to live in both worlds. "Trout" are spiritually immature. Most people assume "trout" are saved, but they are either carp or bass dressed up to look like trout.

There's an age-old, seldom-told story about three ugly troutlings that is similar to the ugly duckling story. As the tale was told by Jay,

> Three little trout were raised in separate ponds.
> Carp ate the first ugly troutling [in the first pond].
> The second ugly troutling [in the second pond] discovered he was a bass. As soon as he realized it, he ate the carp.
> The third ugly troutling [in the third pond] was a carp. But the bass thought he was a trout and didn't eat him. Since the bass thought this, the carp thought he was a trout, too. So the other fish let the carp they thought was a trout live in the pond. He grew up, got married, and had lots of little carp who were raised to think they were trout.
> There were then so many trout that quite a few of the bass wished they could be trout, and began dressing like them. Now there are so many carp who

think they are trout, and so many bass who look like trout, the bass are being squeezed out of the pond. That's what happens when you let a little carp into your pond.

One day the sky that Chicken Little thought was falling actually did fall. All the fish in the third pond were killed.

Carp do not go to fish heaven, but bass do. None of the carp who thought they were trout went. And there weren't many bass left to go . . . There is something fishy in Christendom and I know what it is: Carp.[1]

What are you—a bass, a trout, or a carp? Truly committed disciples (bass) are those who are growing in their faith and service. They sense a call to accountability and responsibility for themselves and others. True believers realize that discipleship requires both an attitude and resulting actions.

Something's Fishy in the Carty Home

Jay grew up in a dysfunctional single-parent home and set out on his own at 14 years of age. He had every right to be bitter. He chose instead to be better.

As Jay hitchhiked across America, he read a Bible that his alcoholic mom had placed in his hands. Little by little, God's Word soaked in, and through others discipling him, he dedicated his life to Christ.

Jay's dad was a professional gambler-bookmaker, and Jay inherited his father's mathematical eye for correlations and probabilities. It was during one of the rare but special times with his dad on a fishing trip in the Sierras that Jay had an opportunity to seriously consider God's provision and protection.

Once a year Jay's dad hired an outfitter to take him and Jay on a pack trip to Lake Wallace. This golden trout lake is located at the 11,500-foot elevation. The nights are brisk and the beautiful orange-bellied trout are awesome.

They drove to the end of the trail and then began to pick their way, by mule, along a narrow rocky ledge for 11 miles into base camp. During the week, fishing was a bit slow, and only a few small fish had graced their orange-colored Flatfish lure. Everyone remembered the year before when fishing had been great with a few trophy three-pounders caught. Empty creels translated into disappointment and frustration.

Discouragement filled the camp as they packed up their gear and the seven mules. The guides headed down the treacherous path dragging the animals behind. In his despair, Jay was not attentive to the saddle that was beginning to loosen on his mount. Suddenly, Jay's dog fell under the mule, the horse shifted, and Jay started pitching toward the shear drop-off. Just as Jay looked down the 400-foot canyon, the guide riding behind him bolted forward, grabbing Jay by his shirttail. With a strong pull, he straightened Jay till he was upright again.

The old rope in the guide's opposite hand—which was attached to the string of pack mules—broke in the struggle. Suddenly the mules bolted toward the two riders. Jay and the guide looked for a place to bail off the trail, but there wasn't one. The angry mules let out a bellow as a collision with the anxious riders seemed imminent and unavoidable.

Just as the mules approached the two, they suddenly stopped and turned around. Jay recalls, "I remember that there was barely enough room for the two of us, let alone seven mules. I still don't know how or why they turned around and headed away from us. It was an absolute miracle."

As the wrangler left Jay to seek out the wayward mules, Jay had some time to reflect on God's mercy and protection. "What are the odds that a well-trained guide would have a worn-out rope connected to the lead animal? I wonder what the probability is that those stubborn mules would turn around on the narrow trail instead of running us over? Wow—this must be divine intervention."

It is trials such this that help us determine what type of "fish" we really are.

What Are the Odds?

Odds also come into play when we consider Jesus' identity. When Jesus asked people to follow Him, He provided undeniable evidence that He was the God-man. Through the testimony of the prophets, His miracles, the presence of the Holy Spirit, the power of God's Word, and His resurrection, Jesus proved His deity.

As Ron Rhodes points out in his book *The Heart of Christianity*, one evidence that proves Jesus is the divine Messiah is that He is the fulfillment of virtually hundreds of messianic prophecies in the Old Testament. This includes prophecies Jesus couldn't possibly have conspired to fulfill, such as His birthplace (Micah 5:2), being born of a virgin (Isaiah 7:14), and the identity of His forerunner, John the Baptist (Malachi 3:1).

Mathematically speaking, there is something like a 1 in 10^{17} (1 in 100,000,000,000,000,000) chance of one man fulfilling just eight of the hundreds of messianic prophecies in the Old Testament. Peter Stoner, the author of *Science Speaks*, provides an illustration to help us understand the magnitude of such odds:

> Suppose that we take 10^{17} silver dollars and lay them on the face of Texas. They will cover all of the state two feet deep. Now mark one of these silver dollars and stir the whole mass thoroughly, all over the state. Blindfold a man and tell him that he can travel as far as he wishes, but he must pick up one silver dollar and say that this is the right one. What chance would he have of getting the right one? Just

the same chance that the prophets would have had of writing these eight prophecies and having them all come true in any one man, from their day to the present time, providing they wrote using their own wisdom.[2]

Discipleship requires an acceptance of Jesus' claims. He was born of a virgin, died on Calvary's cross for our sins, and rose from the dead (1 Corinthians 15:1-4). By turning to Him in repentance and placing our faith in Him, we are saved to a new life (Acts 16:31). To do anything less, we are kidding ourselves and maybe fooling some who know us, but never God.

I have noticed over the years that fishermen and disciples fall into one of several camps:

- Those who think about fishing—*philosophers*.

- Those who study about it and stay at home, never visiting a lake or stream—*scholars*.

- Those who stand on the shore and watch others fish—*observers*.

- Those who go through the motions but believe their equipment isn't really good enough—*pretenders* and *deceivers*.

- Those critical of the whole idea of fishing—*destroyers*.

- Those who write a check to enable others to fish—*sponsors*.

- Those who partake of the meal after the fish are caught—*freeloaders*, *ticks*, and *parasites*.

- Those who pursue the sport with passion and zeal—*disciples*.

What Is a True Disciple?

In my book *Promising Waters*, I devote some 200 pages to describing discipleship and how to practically understand and apply God's teaching on this foundational concept. The biblical Greek word for "disciple" is *mathetes*, which simply means "to learn." Therefore, a disciple is a learner, pupil, or student. [3]

A fisherman teaches his trade to an apprentice one step at a time. Because there are so many variables in fishing, many repetitive sessions are often needed to thoroughly acquaint an angler with all the possible alternatives. Likewise, a disciple learns best by experiencing a teaching through repetition.

A disciple is a leader-in-training. The disciple so identifies with the master's attitudes and actions that he himself becomes a leader. The process begins by receiving Christ as Lord and Savior and becoming a true learner. A disciple is learning, growing, and preparing to teach others as he matures. True discipleship, then, produces growth and evidence of maturity in wisdom and judgment. A disciple is a person-in-process who, through the power of the Holy Spirit, progressively becomes more and more like Christ.

In keeping with this, Jay Carty tells us that "belief that results in salvation embraces repentance, allegiance, and commitment. It's more than just turning from sin; it also includes a drawing alongside of Christ and a desire to do what He says. A person who just 'believes' has a head knowledge of Christ but isn't sold out."[4]

If we are sold out for Jesus and He is our passion, we will want to share our beliefs with others. Discipleship by its nature implies the idea of teaching and encouraging others in their faith. This happens because we make ourselves available and consider every opportunity a time to build a bridge of understanding to the unsaved.

The Ultimate Disciple

Few disciples had more zeal and passion for the lost than did Andrew. We first meet this man in Scripture when he identifies himself as a follower and disciple of John the Baptist. Andrew and John were the first of the 12 to attach themselves to Jesus (*see* John 1:35-39).

No sooner did Andrew discover Jesus for himself than he went to find his brother Peter to bring him to Jesus. Peter became acquainted with Jesus and emerged as the undisputed leader of the apostolic band. Along with James and John, Peter formed an inner circle with their Savior sharing some of His most intimate moments.

Was Andrew envious or resentful? No way! Andrew was unconcerned about who the top dog was. Disciples like him form the backbone of the Christian church and are truly the salt of the earth.

On at least three separate occasions Andrew emerges from the pages of John's Gospel as the consummate crusader whose primary concern was evangelism. He is seen using his fishing background to meet people in the marketplace of life in order to share his faith. He begins by introducing his brother Peter to Jesus (John 1:40-42). On the second occasion he is seen bringing to Jesus the lad with the five loaves and the two fish (John 6:8-9). Andrew was eager to bring *anyone* to Christ, even a little child. On the third occasion we see Andrew doing the work of evangelism when he brings some Greeks to Jesus (John 12:20-22). Evangelism was truly the driving force in Andrew's life.

Discipleship Principles from Brother Andrew

Andrew understood Jesus so well that he knew his Master was never too busy to spend time with those seriously seeking truth. He is never too busy for you or me. He is always there to hear our prayers and provide the inspiration and guidance for our daily living.

Jay Carty realized this as a young desperate boy looking for someone to help strengthen and encourage him. Only Jesus can be the ultimate support and consistent provider-protector.

Andrew's modeling of what it means to be a disciple is worthy of our imitation. There are three primary ways we can follow his lead.

1. *Andrew sought to be unselfish in representing Christ.* He knew that his brother Peter was a natural, instinctive leader. It didn't bother Andrew to take the backseat. He was unconcerned with who got the credit. He was obedient to the call and sought to faithfully spread the word about the Savior. Often this meant that Andrew gave up his own recognition for the sake of honoring others. Scripture later tells us that Andrew was a gifted communicator (Acts 8:5-8) and preached in many lands. He obviously had the ability, but deliberately sought to serve Jesus and encourage others rather than promote himself. Once he proved his faithfulness and loyalty, God gave him a powerful international ministry.

2. *Andrew was an optimist.* The little boy with the five loaves and two fish (John 6:1-13) was seen by Andrew as someone who could be used by Jesus to bless many. It never occurred to Andrew that feeding 5000 people was a hopeless situation. He recognized that Jesus can use anyone to accomplish His miracles. This same optimism is evident in that Andrew sought out the difficult areas of the world to spread the word. Places like Cappadocia, Bithynia, Galatia, and Byzantium were hostile, barbaric lands filled with despair and savage people. Yet Andrew went to these lands with a sense of mission and purpose. His keen insights and optimistic heart greatly impacted these countries for Christ.

3. *Andrew was not prejudiced.* At a time when races and cultures did not mix with one another, Andrew sought to share God's Word with all people (John 12:21). He was universal in his outreach. Most Jews did not believe that another race could possibly have any use to God. Gentiles were considered

an accursed group of people. Andrew was the first of the disciples to realize that Christ's message was for all humankind. He crossed all racial and cultural barriers to present Christ as Lord and Savior to all.

Two Sold-Out Disciples

There is something special about both Andrew and Jay—two disciples separated by thousands of years. Life placed them in positions where they could have been resentful and embittered, but they were well-content being second-string players. Andrew backed up Peter, and Jay backed up Wilt Chamberlain. Both Andrew and Jay were stars in their own right, but sought to place their primary focus on Jesus. They endeavored to glorify Christ and not themselves.

Andrew was committed until the end. He was scourged with rods, fastened to an X-shaped cross, and left to die. It was his wish not to die on the same type of cross as Jesus, for he felt unworthy. This was yet another example of Andrew's humble spirit which consistently sought to glorify Christ.

Andrew lived and died a true disciple and missionary. It is my aspiration, and Jay Carty's, to imitate Andrew in our lives. May we be allowed to die while engaged in the process of bringing others to Christ. *What a way to go!*

Personal Growth

- What fish could best describe your present spiritual nature—a carp, a trout, or a bass?

- If you are a trout (a lukewarm Christian—carp in trout clothing), how can you more fully commit your life to Christ this week?

- How are you representing Christ? Are you concerned about who gets the credit?

• Jesus calls us to discipleship in attitude and action. What action (outreach) have you undertaken? How can you help spread the Word?

PERSONAL PROFILE

Jay Carty

Background—Raised in single-parent home. Played basketball for the Los Angeles Lakers. Coached at UCLA. Founder and President of YES! Ministries, a discipleship outreach program. Has served as a church growth consultant, appeared on numerous radio and television shows, and has authored three books. (You can contact Jay at YES! Ministries, 1033 Newton Rd., Santa Barbara, CA 93103 (805) 962-7579.)

Age When First Fish Caught—Ten years old (a trout at a Sierra lake).

Favorite Bible Verses—Psalm 139:23-24.

Family—Married to Mary for 34 years. One son and daughter.

Favorite Fishing Hole—Wallace Lake, California.

Favorite Fishing Lure—Orange Flatfish.

Preferred Equipment—Spinning.

Most Respected Fishing Pro/Mentor or Instructor—He never had a fishing mentor, but John Wooden was a great inspiration.

Personal Comments—"I thoroughly enjoy the process of helping people say YES to Jesus."

3

The Obedient Disciple

Fishing with Adrian Rogers

It was the 1930s, and times were tough for the Rogers household. The Great Depression bore down on folks like the black plague. Fishing was one sport that experienced a resurgence during this difficult period in history. People visited their local fishing holes more for survival than merely entertainment. Such was the case for the hard-working patriarch of the Rogers family.

Being raised in West Palm Beach, Florida, had its privileges for Adrian and his brother—not the least of which was helping dad catch bluefish off the surf. Both children would catch small bait-fish using pieces of crab or clams. The small fish were rigged on separate rods, then cast into the surf by their dad. The whole family would join in on landing the feisty big fish.

A hastily made campfire and black skillet were all that the three needed to enjoy a good ol' fish fry, with a can of pork and beans to complete the meal. The warm evening sunsets provided a serene backdrop for the family to discuss God's beautiful creation and plan for humankind.

The Call of God

As a young man Adrian felt called to the ministry. His giftedness as an excellent Bible teacher and his obedient heart directed him to serve in several Florida Baptist churches. Each time he was recruited by a church, Adrian carefully measured the call against the direction of the Holy Spirit. His goal was not to become the leader of the largest denomination in the United States, but was rather to understand and obey his Master's leading.

When the First Baptist Church of Merritt Island (Florida) called Adrian, he recognized a unique opportunity to pastor some top scientists and astronauts associated with projects at Cape Kennedy. More importantly, however, he felt God's hand in the placement and accepted the challenge to shepherd this unique congregation.

Adrian recalls those days as being very challenging, with very little time off. "I have never worked so hard. These folks really placed a load on the senior pastor and I tried to respond accordingly."

After about a year and a half, one of the men on staff at the church insisted that Adrian take a break and go fishing. They packed up their gear and drove to a restricted area near the primary launchpad at the Cape. Clearance was given for them to enter a small beach area, where they could wade and fish in the shallow water.

Within minutes each man went his own way, and Adrian started casting a Mirror-Lure with his old Mitchell spinning combo. With the Florida blue sky above and numerous waterbirds filling the air, Adrian soaked up the peace and quiet.

Several hours passed without a single strike. Where were the fish? Each step and cast brought new anticipation, but no success.

Adrian looked up and prayed, "Lord I have tried to be obedient and have sought to faithfully serve you. It would really do my heart good if, out of your kindness, you would grant that I could catch a fish—and any ol' fish will do." As Adrian lowered his head, he spotted a dark, deep pocket just ahead of him. He moved a few steps toward the sinkhole and placed his lure right in the center.

Unsure of the depth, Adrian allowed the lure to settle for several seconds. Then he began to slowly reel. Just as the lure was about to clear the dark hole, he spotted another shadow—moving at a fast rate. The large yellow mouth of a speckled trout opened and engulfed the Mirror-Lure.

The spunky trout took off, peeling several yards of frayed line from the dusty reel. After several runs and some shouts of joy, Adrian wrestled the trophy-size trout ashore. "The thrill and adrenaline rush that comes from such a battle is one of the things that inspires all anglers," Adrian recounts. "It was one of those awesome experiences that you never forget."

Adrian reflects, "I really felt it was more than a coincidence that this fish hit right after I prayed, so I thought I would try it again. I said, 'Lord that was wonderful. I'd really enjoy the experience if you would provide another one of those monster fish for me. If you can guide that miracle fish to the apostle Peter's hook, then I believe you can do the same for me.'"

He made a second cast into the same spot and again allowed the lure to settle. Just like before, the lure came out of the pocket only to be swallowed by another giant trout. The ensuing fight was exciting. Adrian landed the fish right next to the one already beached. "I remember looking around hoping someone would have seen this miracle. But it was just me, God, and two beautiful fish." He thanked God for these gifts and made his way back to his partner to share the joy and blessing.

This event occurred more than 30 years ago. But the sparkle in Adrian's eye as he tells it testifies to the fact that this was no ordinary trip. It was blessed of God. Adrian is a firm believer in the power of prayer and recognizes that God loves His children enough to provide special gifts from time to time. While some may see this as a trivial thing to the God who created the universe, Adrian believes that "God doesn't see things as big or small. He hears the prayers of a small child with the same compassion and care as He listens to a great theologian."

The Obedient Fisherman

In my book *Promising Waters*, I talked briefly about obedience and its practical application in overcoming discouragement. I noted how Jesus took a potentially discouraging day for the disciples (they didn't catch a single fish) and turned it into one of the best fishing days they'd ever seen.

The setting was along the shoreline of the Sea of Galilee. Jesus had been preaching and teaching all over Judea and the Galilee area. He had been rejected by his hometown crowd and moved toward Capernaum where the multitudes seemed to appreciate His teachings.

As you read this wonderful passage of Scripture, look for the numerous times the disciples demonstrated obedience to their Lord:

> One day as Jesus was standing by the Lake of Gennesaret, with the people crowding round him and listening to the word of God, he saw at the water's edge two boats, left there by the fishermen, who were washing their nets. He got into one of the boats, the one belonging to Simon, and asked him to put out a little from shore. Then he sat down and taught the people from the boat.
>
> When he had finished speaking, he said to Simon, "Put out into deep water, and let down the nets for a catch."
>
> Simon answered, "Master, we've worked hard all night and haven't caught anything. But because you say so, I will let down the nets."

When they had done so, they caught such a large number of fish that their nets began to break. So they signaled to their partners in the other boat to come and help them, and they came and filled both boats so full that they began to sink.

When Simon Peter saw this, he fell at Jesus' knees and said, "Go away from me, Lord; I am a sinful man!" For he and all his companions were astonished at the catch of fish they had taken, and so were James and John, the sons of Zebedee, Simon's partners.

Then Jesus said to Simon, "Don't be afraid; from now on you will catch men." So they pulled their boats up on shore, left everything and followed him. (Luke 5:1-11)

Obedient in the Small Things

Although the disciples had had a long day and were tired and discouraged, they followed the requests of their Master. They pushed the boat offshore so Jesus would have a platform to speak. The water reflected and amplified His voice so all could hear.

When Jesus asked them to put out into deeper water and let down their nets, they obeyed. This was a true test of obedience because any fisherman knows that you can't catch fish in the middle of the day in deep water.

Note the progression of trust and obedience in this passage. Jesus didn't ask them right off to go out in the middle of the lake and let down their nets. As they showed their initial willingness to be obedient (allowing Jesus to use a boat for a speaking platform), God continued to direct and bless them. His blessing led to an overwhelming display of gratitude as well as some embarrassment. Peter was so convicted by the miracle that he bowed down and asked to be alone so that he could work through his guilt. But Jesus knew his heart and quickly forgave the disciple for his lack of total trust. The disciples recognized Jesus' deity and now began referring to Him as "Lord" instead of "teacher" as they had in verse 5.

If Peter would have been only partially obedient, he would have missed the wonderful blessing God had in store for him. A good friend of Adrian Rogers, Charles Stanley, suggested we need to "remember that obedience is doing what God says, when He says, and how He says. To be partially obedient is disobedience. You will never know what your life could have been like if you are not totally obedient. Why risk losing a blessing when you can be sure of winning His trust?"[1]

Peter did *what* Jesus said, *when* He said, and *how* He said. You and I are called to do the same.

An Obedient Heart Is a Prayerful Heart

When the disciples asked Jesus, "Lord, teach us to pray," they uttered one of the deepest and most universal cries of humankind (Luke 11:1). Throughout the ages men and women have sought to know God and have instinctively looked to prayer as the conduit through which to dialogue with the Almighty. If we are to be truly obedient disciples, we must learn to be prayerful disciples. Reading Scripture, fellowshipping with other mature believers, and praying form a strong three-legged stool for us to stand upon and reach up to God.

It is interesting to observe the vast amount of literature presently on the bookshelves dealing with prayer. Even tabloids are calling prayer "the most startling and encouraging scientific breakthrough of our era."[2] They obviously haven't been reading their Bibles because this "breakthrough" has been with us for many centuries.

One secular newspaper describes "startling medical evidence" that prayer works: "It can . . . heal and prevent disease." According to recent research by the Princeton Religious Research Center, nine out of ten people say they pray at least occasionally. However, as Billy Graham notes, "Few people have learned how to put prayer to work for them. We have no sense of coming earnestly and expectantly to God—we simply use prayer as a formality."

At the risk of oversimplification, I believe there are four basic types of prayer:

1. *Petitionary prayer* involves coming to God with specific needs that might relate to material possessions, better health, or the needs of others.

2. *Conversational prayer* involves speaking to God in our own words with our own thoughts. Because God is our Father, we can discuss our problems with Him, as if He were our earthly father.

3. *Ritualistic prayer* involves repeating a memorized prayer or reading a prayer from a book. It involves offering worship to God through the thoughts of someone else.

4. *Meditative prayer* involves moving beyond words or deeds to a reflective mind-set. By being still and waiting upon the Lord, He can guide us and provide a tremendous sense of well-being.

An effective prayer life is essential to being an obedient Christian. When you hear Adrian Rogers pray or speak, you become convinced that his wonderful baritone voice must be similar to what Moses may have heard on the mountaintop. However, more important than his rich tonal qualities is his sincere and earnest desire to regularly communicate with the living God.

Dr. Rogers recognizes that prayer is not only the refuge of the weak, it is the reinforcement of the strong. Prayer is not bending God's will to my will, but it is bringing my will into conformity with God's will. He can then work through me.

Prayer should be regular and timely communication with God. If we truly want to experience His best, we must be in constant communication with Him about all things—big or small.

How is your prayer life? Are you enjoying all that God has in store for you? Or are your nets still empty?

Personal Growth

- Are you regularly communicating with the God of the universe?

- Prayer is opening the channels from our emptiness to God's fullness, from our defeat to His victory. How can you appropriate the power that God has in store for you? Read Matthew 6 for some insights.

- What does Psalm 51 say to you about prayer?

PERSONAL PROFILE

Adrian Rogers

Background—Born and raised in West Palm Beach, Florida. Spent a lot of time catching bluefish.

Age When First Fish Caught—Five years old (caught a seven-inch rockfish off a bridge in a saltwater lagoon).

Favorite Bible Verses—Psalm 112:2,3.

Family—Married 45 years to Joyce. Four children (two boys, two girls), eight grandchildren.

Favorite Fishing Hole—Atlantic Ocean.

Favorite Fishing Lure—Mirror Lure.

Preferred Equipment—Spinning.

Most Respected Fishing Pro/Mentor or Instructor—Bill Dance.

Personal Comments—"There is something about getting into a boat and leaving the shore that is very therapeutic. It is as if the shore represents responsibilities and other things. When you leave, you are in another world."

The Determined Disiciple

Fishing with James Robison

Fishing—The art of casting, trolling, jigging, or spinning while freezing, sweating, swatting, or swearing.

Fishing has always been more than just a sport. It originated about the same time as hunting as a means of attaining food for survival. From the beginning, this pastime has been one that requires great determination.

One of the best fishing stories I've heard about a determined fisherman comes from our forty-first president, George Bush. During an August 1989 fishing vacation in Maine, President Bush went catchless for 17 straight days. The eyes of the entire nation followed the saga as reporters, photographers, and fishermen watched the president's every move in his 28-foot boat.

The press declared a "fish watch" and used a graphic of a bluefish with a red line through it to indicate each "zero fish" day. Reporters were seen wearing improvised press credentials with a "no fish" logo. Several local fishermen and members of the press following the president would, on occasion, proudly wave *their* catches before the envious George Bush.

On the eighteenth day of his vacation, as a last resort, the president appealed to divine intervention by praying at St. Ann's Episcopal Church. That day he caught a ten-pound bluefish on a jawbuster lure. Reporters, staff, the Secret Service, and local fishermen in nearby boats cheered the persistent fisherman. Back at the dock, he was greeted with a hero's welcome for his triumph over a lone bluefish.

President Bush's story reminds us that determination is a key component of success in fishing, just as it is in character building. About eight decades ago, an equally committed president, Grover Cleveland, described the virtue of such determination:

> It is impossible to avoid the conclusion that the fishing habit, by promoting close association with nature, by teaching patience, and by generating or stimulating useful contemplation, tends directly to the increase of the intellectual power of its votaries and through them to the improvement of our national character.[1]

A well-known Christian leader-fisherman who exemplifies determination is James Robison. Robison is a nationally known evangelist and missionary to thousands abroad. His courageous life demonstrates the type of character that is a by-product of being a determined warrior. As the following will make clear, Robison's character was forged in the school of adversity.

A Tough Childhood

Life had been particularly tough for James Robison's mother. She was a hardworking nurse who had rented a room from a family in Houston, Texas. One night the owner's son forced his way into her room and raped her. The result was an unwanted pregnancy. The 41-year-old woman decided the best way to escape her situation was to abort the fetus.

After consulting with a few physicians, she was persuaded instead to carry the child and offer it up for adoption. She put an ad in the newspaper and received a response from a Reverend and Mrs. Hale from Pasadena, Texas. This loving and caring couple adopted her son, James, and raised him with love and care until he was five years old.

At this time in his life, James's mother, who had never granted final custody to the Hales, brought him home to live with her. Unfortunately, she hadn't much to offer her little boy. And they lived in a very poor neighborhood where James was regularly preyed upon by local bullies.

Robison recalls very few positives about his younger years. But it was during this time that he developed a compelling sense of competition in both sports and school. He wasn't a great student, but he loved to read. "The teacher had a bookworm program going in fourth grade. Somehow, in the midst of all that reading, I developed some skills and even some admirable qualities."[2]

For the most part, Robison experienced a sad and miserable childhood. "At the time I was so despondent, and felt so worthless, that many nights I cried and cried," Robison recalls. "I figured I was a bad boy, and that must account for why I never got any breaks. No dad. No friends. No loved ones who remembered me. Sometimes, when I was home alone, I banged my head against the wall until I knocked myself out. I just wanted to escape."[3]

Amidst all the negative circumstances, though, a few rays of sunshine managed to break through in James's early years. He speaks fondly of his first exposure to nature, crediting his present avocation to a certain woman who invested in him at a young age.[4] "Today I am a hunter and a conservationist because Timbo (a one-time housemate) gave of her own time to take me into the woods as a little boy. Somehow,

she knew it was in me to want to spend time in the great outdoors. Hunting and fishing with her provided some of the
most pleasant experiences of my childhood."[5]

A New Direction Emerges

After high school, while attending a weeklong religious
revival, Robison says he listened to the preaching, but felt he
was so far from God's ideal. Nevertheless, God's love managed to break through. "As I sat there, night after night, God
was speaking to me, drawing me closer and closer to Himself."

It was then that James received a direct call from God,
whom he claims specifically told him to become an evangelist. "I knew God had called me. Beyond a shadow of a
doubt, I fell so in love with Jesus that my heart overflowed.
From that moment I had courage and compassion and zeal
without measure. I didn't even have anywhere to preach, but
I was ready. I was willing. And because of God alone, I was
able."[6]

Robison's first preaching experience came at a lunchbreak
he shared with 200 other laborers as he stood atop a flatbed
trailer. He could hardly believe his ears as he began to share
the love of Christ with these lost men whose minds were cor-
rupt and filthy. "As the words tumbled out, I felt a boldness
come over me, a sense of clarity of mind. I wasn't worried
about what people thought of me. I was preaching!"[7]

God didn't let James quit with those 200 laborers. Soon
he was preaching nationwide. "In one way, of course, I was
not myself at all. If it had been *me* accepting those speaking
invitations all over Texas and Louisiana, I would have stood
before those people looking down at the floor, shuffling my
feet, and mumbling. I was still shy and withdrawn. But when
God gave me holy boldness, and taught me to use gestures,
balance, and voice inflection, I became a different person in
the pulpit. I felt comfortable. I stepped into the pulpit with

confidence and righteous indignation over sin. I was forceful about the truths from the Word of God and emotional over the lost."[8]

Success God's Way

Robison overcame many hurdles to achieve success, including chronic physical ailments. "Every morning I had to go through a painful stretching exercise just to loosen those muscles so I could move about during the day. It was awful. I accepted it as a way of life."[9] But these physical problems didn't deter him from his work of ministry. And his ministry continued to attain more and more success.

At a point in James's career, the business of ministry began to undermine the godliness befitting a servant. It took a strong nudge from the Holy Spirit to remind him of a key to true success. "We thought nothing could stop us or even slow us down. Little did I realize that I had allowed the enemy an inroad: I was too busy, too successful for the intimate, personal devotion time with Jesus."[10]

It was then that James learned that coming beside restful waters to be refreshed and loved by the Lord is the secret of perseverance and true success. He began to pray that his desires would never again get in the way of God's will for his life. He pleaded with the Lord to remind him of his promise to always come back to Him in private, where it was just him and the Lord, loving each other.

Calling Upon the Heavenly Father

James recalls that while growing up there were precious few people who wanted to take a disenfranchised boy out fishing. "As my relationship grew with God, I realized he was the father I never had. He cared about what I cared about. He liked to see me have fun. I regularly called upon Him for help in finding fish. He certainly knew what area of the lake to send Peter (Matthew 17:27), and what side of the boat to tell the disciples to throw their nets (John 21:6)."

James remembers one occasion in particular when he had just finished a long and difficult mission trip to Africa. He decided to take a day off and go fishing. "Even though it was in the middle of summer and in the heat of the day, I felt confident," James reflects. "As I launched my boat I felt like I heard the Lord tell me, 'James you did good. I know it was a hard trip. So now I want you to take your boat and go left, right through that little passageway, and cast over there by that little stump.' "

With a smile, James recalls that "as my worm was sinking, I felt that 'thud.' I set the hook and this bass came out of the water spitting and sputtering. His mouth looked like a toilet bowl. We played tug-of-war for a while. Then I scooped up this monster fish that weighed 11.2 pounds. As I was admiring the fish, I felt like I heard the Lord say, 'How did you like that?' "

We learn a good lesson from James Robison: *Determination pays off!* God blesses and smiles upon the efforts of His determined servants. Whether fishing for fish or fishing for souls, determination is a key ingredient in the recipe for success.

Personal Growth

• Has God ever asked you to do something you didn't feel qualified to do? Did you sense His empowering?

• What hurdles of pain and circumstances has God helped you to overcome?

• Have you found that in times alone with God, "coming beside restful waters," you find the peace and strength you need to persevere?

PERSONAL PROFILE

James Robison

Background—Born in Houston, Texas. Raised by adoptive parents in Pasadena, Texas. Has conducted over 600 citywide crusades attended by more than 15 million people. He is a televangelist with an international ministry to millions of disadvantaged youngsters around the world.

Age When First Fish Caught—Two years old (a speckled trout in the Gulf). Reverend and Mrs. Hale had to tie a rope to James's suspenders to keep him in the boat.

Favorite Bible Verse—John 12:32.

Family—Married to Betty. Two daughters and a son.

Favorite Fishing Hole—Anywhere a bass will bite (especially Lake Guerro, Mexico).

Favorite Fishing Lure—Zara Spook, Plastic Worm.

Preferred Equipment—Bait Casting.

Most Respected Fishing Pro/Mentor or Instructor—Jimmy Houston and Bill Dance.

Personal Comments—"I've been at the bottom. I know what it is to fail, and I've hated myself for my failures. But God gave me the grace to forgive myself and the grace to forgive others. He healed me, and restored me. The good news is that it can happen to you."

5

Living Under Grace

Fishing with Norm Evans

Norm Evans, a former all-pro offensive tackle, is one busy guy. His Pro Athletes Outreach (PAO) boasts some 7000 members made up of Christian athletes from a variety of sports. Norm and his wife Bobbe have run the 27-year-old organization since June 1984. They realized that thousands of active and retired athletes and their spouses needed help in finding lasting solutions for the intense pressures that develop with a career in professional sports.

PAO is a Christian leadership training ministry that requires teamwork and dynamic leadership, as well as determination. Norm's leadership skills developed during his years of professional football. He established himself as one of the league's top offensive right tackles while playing for the world champion Miami Dolphins. His leadership skills and directive approach to problem-solving helped keep him in professional sports for 14 years.

As is the case with most leaders, it is hard for Norm to turn off the motors when he settles in at home. I know what it's like, because some of the tendencies Norm admits to also played out in my family. There is a tendency to overmanage our homes and create pressure that can sometimes present problems for those we love most. Fortunately, Norm's wife Bobbe is one sharp lady with a strong temperament to help throttle some of the stress associated with her driven husband.

The pressures of managing a national ministry and counseling with many celebrity athletes are great. To help alleviate some of this pressure, Norm annually takes his son Ron on a fishing trip to HiHium Lake near Cache Creek, British Columbia. This pristine little lake has served as "home away from home" for Norm and a group of his friends who make a yearly pilgrimage to this "little piece of heaven."

The rustic 70-year-old cabins, with their old wooden boats, look like something out of a Thomas Kinkade painting. The 5000' elevation keeps the nights cold and the fish active. Each morning these fathers and their sons would cook up a hearty country breakfast and talk about who was going to catch the biggest fish.

Every year Norm and his son would venture off to their secret place that allowed them to take some time for really appreciating one another. It was during one of these annual trips that Norm realized the importance of relinquishing some of his authority to young Ron. "During each trip I tried to encourage Ron to make the decisions. I let him pick the boat, select the lures, and move the boat to just the right spot. It was important for him to develop leadership skills, knowing that each choice could spell either success or failure. Either way, he would have my blessing and love."

On a typical late June day, near the end of a weeklong trip, Norm had a chance to weave into the fabric of Ron's life the values and traditions that inspire real faith. One of the other dads had caught a jumbo 24.5-inch Kamloop trout. "This guy was really rubbing our nose in his apparent victory," Norm said. "He and his son were carrying on about how they finally beat us.

"As soon as Ron and I finished dinner, we packed up our gear and hurried to get down to the far end of the lake," recalls Norm. "Ron just felt confident about fishing that part of the lake, even though we hadn't fished it all week."

Norm put out a wet fly on one of his ultra-light rods. And out of nowhere he got slammed. "It was like a linebacker hit me."

Suddenly the fight was on. A large fish surfaced and all you could see in the evening shadows were fins and a large wake as the fish made its way back toward the cove. "My heart was in my throat as Ron yelled out, 'Dad it's as big as a salmon!' He was so excited."

Norm and his son fought the fish until just before dark when they managed to net the monster. The fish was immediately brought in and the celebration began. It measured exactly one-sixteenth of an inch *larger* than his buddy's fish. It was unbelievable.

Besides teaching Ron how to make decisions, a key lesson Norm tried to instill in him during these trips was the importance of grace in our lives. Norm reflects, "While a young lad's decisions on a big fishing trip may not rank on the top ten list of critical decisions for life, the trips were an opportunity for me to show him that grace (or unmerited favor) was a natural thing because he was my son and I loved him. He would make a poor decision and look at me with those big eyes and say, 'Sorry, Dad!' My love and appreciation for him grew greater each time he realized his failures and corrected his actions. And when I admit my mistakes and failures to him, he has always been quick to forgive me."

It was good and right for Norm to allow Ron the freedom to make mistakes and feel his father's comforting acceptance and grace. The competitive environments of our stress-filled world don't usually provide an atmosphere conducive to reflective thinking and patience. The undisturbed atmosphere of this little lake was like an incubation chamber for the attribute of grace—a place where soft words could be spoken and godly ideas hatched into life.

Of course, the very anchor to our salvation is the grace of God: "By grace you have been saved" (Ephesians 2:8). Because God is gracious, sinful human beings can be forgiven. It is not because of anything in them that they are saved. It is only because of the boundless love, goodness, pity, compassion, mercy, and grace of God.

Amazing Grace

Having spent considerable time visiting various churches as a guest speaker, I'm convinced that most folks really don't understand this fundamental doctrine of the Christian faith. I see many church leaders that are quick to discuss the importance of fearing God and obeying His every command. Many believers are quick to remind others that God is watching their every move and that followers "better watch out—God will get you." It is no wonder that those who have not yet received Jesus as their personal Savior are not interested in pursuing such a threatening faith.

Those legalistic, judgmental believers who often set the rules and interpret the ordinances are really no better than the first-century Pharisees and Sadducees. By their attitudes and actions, they are grace-killers. Most of the time these folks miss out on the joy of their faith because they are too worried about messing up.

Jesus came to set us free, to release us for service. He desires us to enjoy our faith and live the abundant life (John 10:10). The Protestant Reformation (fifteenth century) was all about a group of people who realized that Christianity should be built upon grace, not upon guilt. In fact, grace is foundational for faith itself. "No man can come to me, except the Father which hath sent me draw him" (John 6:44 KJV).

The very act of the Father drawing us and encouraging us to have faith is an indication of His grace.

See if you can detect God's grace in the following verses:

Consequently, just as the result of one trespass was condemnation for all men, so also the result of one act of righteousness was justification that brings life for all men. For just as through the disobedience of the one man the many were made sinners, so also through the obedience of the one man the many will be made righteous. (Romans 5:18-19)

For God so loved the world that he gave his one and only Son, that whoever believes in him shall not perish but have eternal life. (John 3:16)

Coming to faith—being accepted into the family of God for all eternity—can't be that simple, can it? *It is* that simple! That's why we call it God's grace (unmerited favor). Do I mean that all you have to do is believe that Jesus died for your sins, ask Him to forgive you of those transgressions, receive Him as Lord of your life, and you're saved? Yep! That's what God's Word teaches and that's why it's called heavenly grace.

One author describes the life of grace this way:

Living in grace means that we express His life as a natural and normal part of our daily experience. We live trusting Him to express Himself through us every day. We don't have to overanalyze our actions and attitudes. Life isn't a test, it's a rest. The test has already been given and we received a perfect score because Jesus took the test for us. It's time now to celebrate! We don't need to live under a list of things we believe we ought to do. When we are living each day abiding in Christ, we can do whatever we want to. As we abide in Him, His desire will be our desire.[1]

The Undeserved Gift

What is grace all about? Other than the Bible, there is probably no more comprehensive work to describe grace than Chuck Swindoll's masterpiece, *The Grace Awakening*. Many of my impressions, actions, and attitudes about myself and others were formed from his insightful teachings on this subject. Consider his words:

> To show grace is to extend favor or kindness to one who doesn't deserve it and can never earn it. Receiving God's acceptance by grace always stands in sharp contrast to earning it on the basis of works. Every time the thought of grace appears, there is the idea of its being undeserved. In no way is the recipient getting what he or she deserves. Favor is being extended simply out of the goodness of the heart of the giver. . . . It is absolutely and totally free. You will never be asked to pay it back. You couldn't even if you tried.[2]

There are literally hundreds of verses in Scripture that describe grace and encourage us to be disciples of grace. Read slowly just a few of these, and then ask yourself if you have truly accepted the grace God has given you: "The law was given by Moses, but grace and truth came by Jesus Christ" (John 1:17 KJV). "By grace you have been saved, through faith" (Ephesians 2:8). "Where sin abounded, grace did much more abound" (Romans 5:20 KJV). "I am astonished that you are so quickly deserting the one who called you by the grace of Christ and are turning to a different gospel" (Galatians 1:6).

Is this a one-time deal? Salvation is, but not grace. God's sustaining mercy, compassion, leniency, and forgiveness are ongoing for all who believe. He continually empowers and strengthens us through His giving of grace. James D. Mallory, Jr. states, "Many Christians seem to understand the concept of being saved by grace, but they have missed the concept of being sustained by grace."[3]

God's greatest example of grace was His Christmas gift to humankind. From a Christmas card I've saved is this message that captures the spirit of God's grace in sending His Son:

> If our greatest need had been information,
> God would have sent us an educator.
> If our greatest need had been technology,
> God would have sent us a scientist.
> If our greatest need had been money,
> God would have sent us an economist.
> If our greatest need had been pleasure,
> God would have sent us an entertainer.
> But our greatest need was forgiveness,
> so God sent us a Savior!

"I'm Just Not Good Enough"

For those of you about ready to turn to a new chapter in this book because you feel your actions and attitudes are not worthy of grace, I encourage you to read on. Because God is gracious, sinful human beings can be forgiven and saved. It is not because of anything they do, but is because of the infinite love, mercy, compassion, and grace of God.

How big is the grace of God? Who can measure its breadth? Who can fathom its depth? As with all other divine attributes, God's dispersion of grace is infinite and never-ending.

Have you persecuted, tortured, and killed believers? Have you blasphemed the very name of our Lord? Sounds pretty bad, right? Could God really forgive someone who did all that? Yes, He could *and He did*. And He did so because of this grace.

Following is a quick summary of Paul's life (formerly called "Saul the persecutor"):

For I am the least of the apostles and do not even deserve to be called an apostle, because I persecuted the church of God. But by the grace of God I am what I am, and His grace to me was not without effect. No, I worked harder than all of them—yet not I, but the grace of God that was with me. Whether, then, it was I or they, this is what we preach, and this is what you believed. (1 Corinthians 15:9-11)

So, if you're ever tempted to think you're not good enough, just remember the apostle Paul. He wasn't good enough either. None of us are. That's why God gives us His grace.

Living a Life of Grace

Donald Grey Barnhouse, the late pastor and Bible scholar, said, "Love that goes upward is worship; love that goes outward is affection; love that stoops is grace."[4] Living a life of grace in our critical culture is not always easy. Our driven society is one that fosters perfectionism. But nobody is perfect.

If a professional baseball player gets a hit once every three times up at bat, we place him in the hall of fame. If a basketball player shoots 50 percent, he will likely make the Dream Team. If a quarterback has more touchdown passes than interceptions, ESPN will be interviewing him on a regular basis.

Yet, in our own lives, and often in the attitude we project to others, we demand a smothering kind of control. By our failure to show grace, we sometimes cultivate a sense of discouragement and fear in people. Occasionally, we intimidate others through our position or power. We may become more concerned about getting credit and receiving glory rather than focusing on opportunities to encourage others. We may lack the spontaneity to try another person's ideas for fear that our own may not look quite as good. Maybe someone has offended us and we just can't forgive him or her for his or her trespass.

When we operate with these judgmental, legalistic attitudes, we lack grace in our lives. Grace is kind and gentle, always willing to quickly forgive and encourage. Grace is always the better way.

A Lesson from Haggai and Zechariah

Tucked away in a duet of small Old Testament books are the profiles of two men, Haggai and Zechariah. These were ancient prophets who lived and wrote during a Renaissance time in Israel. To help understand their mission and passion, let's first set the stage for their appearance.

Jerusalem lay in ruins. It was nothing more than a pile of rubble. Everything had been torched or leveled. The chosen people had been living in captivity in the distant land of Babylon. After seven decades, some of the more faithful began to make their way back to Zion. Nehemiah led the first group back to build the outer wall of the temple.

Many of these folks became sidetracked, however, with rebuilding their homes. None were all that interested in resurrecting the temple. They were tired and defeated. They were content to just retire in their partially restored community.

Haggai was a single-minded prophet with a strong, severe, and pungent management style. With criticism and sarcasm, he prodded the Israelites to begin rebuilding the temple. His persistent harassment was discouraging and uninspiring to the people of that day. A serious depression settled over the land as this driver-authoritarian personality did nothing to motivate the Israelites into action.

Zerubbabel was the governor during these difficult times. He had been assigned the task of rebuilding the temple. He relied on the prophets and religious leaders to inspire the labors. When the building project seemed impossible to the frustrated governor, the prophet Zechariah came along.

Zechariah was an encourager. He had vision and a passion—passion not only for the project but for the people. His gracious approach inspired and motivated the people. The Lord looked with favor upon the man and the mission, and stirred the people and the governor to action. People soon got excited about the vision of their holy place.[5]

The Spirit of God was upon the taskmaster as well as the task at hand. To emphasize the importance of grace in this mission, the Lord God sent an angel to Zerubbabel as a timeless reminder that God works best through gracious people, not through the might and power of impetuous leaders.

> So he said to me, "This is the word of the LORD to Zerubbabel: 'Not by might nor by power, but by my Spirit,' says the LORD Almighty. 'What are you, O mighty mountain? Before Zerubbabel you will become level ground. Then he will bring out the capstone to shouts of "God bless it! God bless it!"'" (Zechariah 4:6-7).

The final assurance God provides to Zerubbabel and to all of us who need to continue trusting in Him is found in Zechariah 4:7: "Therefore no mountain, however high, can stand before Zerubbabel! For it will flatten out before him! And Zerubbabel will finish building this Temple with mighty shouts of thanksgiving for God's mercy, declaring that all was done by grace alone" (TLB).

Grace Alone

Grace alone, my friend. *That* is what Norm and Ron's fishing trips to British Colombia were all about. Each trip was a testing ground for Norm to release his son from the demands, expectations, and structure of their daily routine. It was a time for a father to demonstrate his genuine love and support of his son.

Did Ron make mistakes? Sure he did. And Norm allowed him the grace to learn from them.

These trips were also a learning experience for Norm. Four lessons stand out:

1. We can accomplish much through might and power, but it is *more lasting* to employ the Holy Spirit as our partner so that the product and results are of Him.

2. Rather than being critical, be expectant. Provide a lot of encouragement and grace to others.

3. Be more tolerant and less judgmental. Don't be legalistic. Let's reach others with love and compassion.

4. Don't let a person's petty habits or attitudes get in the way of showing them grace.

John Newton's eighteenth-century hymn, "Amazing Grace," continues to be my favorite hymn. The power of Newton's testimony and release from sin grips my soul each time I sing it. Have you experienced God's grace? Are you providing that same grace to others?

> Amazing grace! how sweet the sound!
> That saved a wretch like me!
> I once was lost, but now am found;
> Was blind, but now I see.
> 'Twas grace that taught my heart to fear,
> And grace my fears relieved.
> How precious did that grace appear
> The hour I first believed![6]

Personal Growth

• Have you received the Christmas gift of God's grace? If not, what stands in your way? Remember, "Since we have been justified through faith, we have peace with God through our Lord Jesus Christ" (Romans 5:1).

• Legalistic people tend to project guilt instead of grace. How does Galatians 1:6-10 inspire you?

• How can you be a person of more grace and power? (Read Acts 6:8.)

• What are some lessons of grace you learned from Haggai and Zechariah?

PERSONAL PROFILE

Norm Evans

Background—Born and raised in Santa Fe, New Mexico. Was an outstanding athlete who dedicated himself to Christ and football. Played professional football for 14 years with the Houston Oilers, Miami Dolphins, and Seattle Seahawks.

Age When First Fish Caught—Five years old.

Favorite Bible Verses—1 Corinthians 1:4-9.

Family—Wife, Bobbe. Two children (son and daughter), and one grandchild.

Favorite Fishing Hole—Florida Everglades.

Favorite Fishing Lure—Plastic Worms.

Preferred Equipment—Ultra Light.

Most Respected Fishing Pro/Mentor or Instructor—Jack Kerns.

Personal Comments—"Quality time comes out of quantity of time."

6

Living by Faith

Fishing with Lowell Lundstrom

When we think of people of great faith, names like Abraham, Moses, Nehemiah, Job, and Daniel come to mind. These men demonstrated tremendous trust and dependence on the unseen. Their confidence in God and His promises developed in them character that inspired others and led nations to achieve great success.

In similar fashion, fishermen are by nature people of faith. Who else would leave a nice warm bed early in the morning, drive three hours to a brush-covered mountain stream, crawl on the belly like a reptile to avoid being seen, only to throw the first cast into the top of a tree, thereby spooking the only fish within miles? We do it because we believe the next cast just might produce the fish of a lifetime.

To what degree are fishermen committed to their passion? They are known for losing track of time as they try "just one more spot" before quitting. A person with great faith but little experience, however, may *never* stop fishing once they start. Following are a few rules of thumb that will help you know when it's time to stop fishing:

- The bait is larger than the fish you caught.

- Your four-year-old is playing boats by throwing sticks in the stream and you find out that one of them was your brand-new (and very expensive) fishing pole.

- You fall asleep in your boat only to wake up being hailed in Japanese.

- Every member of your son's Cub Scout troop catches more fish than you do, and they are using bubblegum for bait.

- The motor on your boat gets stuck and you ram the presidential yacht. The Secret Service is convinced you're a spy.

- The best catch of the day was a tire off a '57 Edsel.

- Your lure attracts the creature from the Black Lagoon.

- The marlin you hook hijacks you to Cuba.

- Your line becomes caught on a passing speedboat and you win first place in a waterskiing contest.

- The mosquitoes are bigger than the fish.

- Someone discovers gold in the secret spot you've been fishing for 15 years.

- You didn't pack food for the trip because you promised your family they could easily live on what you caught, and your wife's trying to find recipes that use soda pop cans.

- You get up at 4 A.M., drive 50 miles to your favorite spot only to find a Hell's Angels convention there.

- You down a Coke from the cooler and find instead that you just drank your son's pickled crawdad collection.

- You lose your balance, are swept downstream, and when you wash ashore, it's on the beach where the Fish and Game wardens are holding their annual picnic—and you dropped your license, but not your pole.

- Taking a break for nature's relief, you find yourself surrounded by the local bird-watching club.

- As you hook a fly in your hat, you remember you weren't wearing one.

A Modern Man of Faith

When I think of modern-day men of faith, Lowell Lundstrom is certainly one who comes to mind. For more than 40 years, Lowell has faithfully served God as an evangelist, Bible teacher, and musician. His multifaceted ministry features members of his family who serve with a joy and enthusiasm that is contagious. His dedication and reliance on Jesus is projected in every phase of his life. To hear Lowell speak about the ongoing miracles that continue to bless his life and ministry is awe-inspiring.

Lowell brings that same type of faith along on every fishing trip he takes. Every cast is made with an expectation and confidence that he'll catch a fish.

Lowell's favorite fishing tale relates to a trip he took to Lake Winnipeg River. It had been some time since Lowell and his son, Lowell, Jr. (L.J.), had an opportunity to get away and experience the great outdoors. On their way to the river they stopped by a local tackle shop to do a little browsing.

L.J. spotted a very large minnow-shaped, shallow-running lure. He showed it to his dad and asked him to buy it for their trip. The lure was decked out in all kinds of colors with black, white, and red polkadots scattered all over the body. Lowell was initially less than enthusiastic about spending money on a lure that was probably too big and gaudy looking for the weary muskie. But the persistence of a young boy and the curiosity of an old fisherman was more than tempting. They left the store with expectant hearts and enthusiasm for what God would do.

They fished for several days, catching a few each day. Then, on the last day, things really slowed down. In fact, fishing was so slow that the only way they were going to catch a fish was if the fish happened to yawn while their lure was passing by. Now that's slow.

With just a few minutes of daylight left, Lowell looked down at his old tackle box. He had tried virtually every lure in his box. Well—*almost* every lure. That big, bright, polka-dotted one that L.J. had picked up in the store was still sitting there in its package.

Lowell said to L.J., "Son, you did such a good job of picking out this lure, I want to use it just to see how it works." Lowell picked up the long-bodied lure and snapped it onto his lightweight spinning rod. His cast traveled forever pulling the eight-pound test line with it. As the lure landed next to a shoreline weed bed, there was a sudden splash. "It sounded as if someone dropped a concrete block into the river." And then the action began.

Lowell remembers, "I couldn't see what was on the line as darkness was just settling in, but the line began to stretch off the spool. I knew I had to be very careful and treat this big fellow tenderly as the eight-pound line was beginning to sing out in the damp night air."

The fish finally left the shore and began to circle the small fishing boat. Time and time again it ran laterally as it attempted to free itself from the colorful hunk of wood protruding from its mouth. "It took about 30 to 40 minutes to get the fish close enough to the boat to see what I had. The big eyes of the trophy muskie looked up at me as if to threaten my dominance," Lowell recalls.

L.J. grabbed a small aluminum net and slid it under the fish. As he began to lift it out of the water, the net broke off at the handle. L.J. quickly grabbed the rim with the fish floundering in the netting and lifted the monster into the bottom of the boat.

After some celebrating, the two proud fishermen made their way back to the marina where a number of envious onlookers came over to see the catch. Lowell recalls, "I was very proud of the fish, but even more proud of my son's faith in me and that oversized lure." The 23-pound muskie was mounted into a glass coffee table as a beautiful piece of art and a constant reminder of what faith can accomplish.

Each time Lowell thinks about that adventure, he says he is reminded that "fishermen spend their whole lifetime searching for the really big fish—you know, that storybook fish. I feel the greatest adventure in life is to discover God. If we would search for God as diligently as we troll for fish, we would find that He is the biggest catch in the universe."

Faith Is Our Foundation

From the beginning of time, God has asked human beings to believe in Him. Faith is so important that it is mentioned more than 300 times in Scripture. There is nothing more essential to the Christian than faith.

Faith is believing—believing in the object of our trust, who is God Almighty. As Pastor Ed Hindson, author of *Men of the Promise*, puts it,

> The power of our faith rests in the object of our faith. At the foundation of all love is a belief in the object that is loved. If I do not believe in a person, I cannot love him. The same is true in our relationship with God. Without faith it is impossible for us to know Him and love Him. Faith is the starting point in our spiritual journey. We must begin with God: believing that He exists, believing that He cares, and believing that His love is real.[1]

When you think about it, we have faith in lots of things. We have faith that the sun will come up in the morning, that after the long winter, spring will come, and faith in the miracle of birth. Why not have faith in the God who created it all?

The Rock of Our Salvation

The apostle Paul affirmed, "We live by faith, not by sight" (2 Corinthians 5:7). The reason we can live by faith is that God Himself *is faithful*.

I keep a little journal in the front part of my Bible to remind me of God's faithfulness. It is easy to forget how faithful God has been unless we regularly review His past accomplishments. My journal motivates me to trust and obey His commands and promises both now and in the future.

In a similar fashion, the book of Hebrews lays out the faithfulness of God for all generations to see. Eugene Peterson has developed a unique modern-day paraphrase of the New Testament called *The Message*. Read along with me the wonderful story of faith from the eleventh chapter of Hebrews:

> The fundamental fact of existence is that this trust in God, this faith, is the firm foundation under everything that makes life worth living. It's our handle on what we can't see. The act of faith is what distinguished our ancestors, set them above the crowd.
>
> By faith, we see the world called into existence by God's word, what we see was created by what we don't see.
>
> By an act of faith, Abel brought a better sacrifice to God than Cain. It was what he *believed*, not what he brought, that made the difference. That's what God noticed and approved as righteous. After all these centuries, that belief continues to catch our notice.

By an act of faith, Enoch skipped death completely. "They looked all over and couldn't find him because God had taken him." We know on the basis of reliable testimony that before he was taken "he pleased God." It's impossible to please God apart from faith. And why? Because anyone who wants to approach God must believe both that he exists *and* that he cares enough to respond to those who seek him.

By faith, Noah built a ship in the middle of dry land. He was warned about something he couldn't see, and acted on what he was told. The result? His family was saved. His act of faith drew a sharp line between the evil of the unbelieving world and the rightness of the believing world. As a result, Noah became intimate with God.

By an act of faith, Abraham said yes to God's call to travel to an unknown place that would become his home. When he left he had no idea where he was going. By an act of faith he lived in the country promised him, lived as a stranger camping in tents. Isaac and Jacob did the same, living under the same promise. Abraham did it by keeping his eye on an unseen city with real, eternal foundations—the City designed and built by God.

By faith, barren Sarah was able to become pregnant, old woman as she was at the time, because she believed the One who made a promise would do what he said. That's how it happened that from one man's dead and shriveled loins there are now people numbering into the millions.

Each one of these people of faith died not yet having in hand what was promised, but still believing. How did they do it? They saw it way off in the distance, waved their greeting, and accepted the fact that they were transients in this world. People who live this way make it plain that they are looking for their true home. If they were homesick for the old country, they could have gone back any time they wanted. But they were after a far better country than that—heaven country. You can see why God is so proud of them, and has a City waiting for them.

By faith, Abraham, at the time of testing, offered Isaac back to God. Acting in faith, he was as ready to return the promised son, his only son, as he had been to receive him and this after he had already been told, "Your descendants shall come from Isaac." Abraham figured that if God wanted to, he could raise the dead. In a sense, that's what happened when he received Isaac back, alive from off the altar.

By an act of faith, Isaac reached into the future as he blessed Jacob and Esau.

By an act of faith, Jacob on his deathbed blessed each of Joseph's sons in turn, blessing them with God's blessing, not his own—as he bowed worshipfully upon his staff.

By an act of faith, Joseph, while dying, prophesied the exodus of Israel, and made arrangements for his own burial.

By an act of faith, Moses' parents hid him away for three months after his birth. They saw the child's beauty, and they braved the king's decree.

By faith, Moses, when grown, refused the privileges of the Egyptian royal house. He chose a hard life with God's people rather than an opportunistic soft life of sin with the oppressors. He valued suffering in the Messiah's camp far greater than Egyptian wealth because he was looking ahead, anticipating the payoff. By an act of faith, he turned his heel on Egypt, indifferent to the king's blind rage. He had his eye on the One no eye can see, and kept right on going. By an act of faith, he kept the Passover Feast and sprinkled Passover blood on each house so that the destroyer of the firstborn wouldn't touch them.

By an act of faith, Israel walked through the Red Sea on dry ground. The Egyptians tried it and drowned.

By faith, the Israelites marched around the walls of Jericho for seven days, and the walls fell flat.

By an act of faith, Rahab, the Jericho harlot, welcomed the spies and escaped the destruction that came on those who refused to trust God.

I could go on and on, but I've run out of time. There are so many more—Gideon, Barak, Sanison, Jephthah, David, Samuel, the prophets. . . . Through acts of faith, they toppled kingdoms, made justice work, took the promises for themselves. They were protected from lions, fires, and sword thrusts, turned disadvantage to advantage, won battles, routed alien armies. Women received their loved ones back from the dead. There were those who, under torture, refused to give in and go free, preferring something better: resurrection. Others braved abuse and whips, and, yes, chains and dungeons. We have stories of those who were stoned, sawed in two, murdered in cold blood; stories of vagrants wandering the earth in animal skins, homeless, friendless, powerless—the world didn't deserve them!—making their way as best they could on the cruel edges of the world.

Not one of these people, even though their lives of faith were exemplary, got their hands on what was promised. God had a better plan for us: that their faith and our faith would come together to make one completed whole, their lives of faith not complete apart from ours.

Everything Is Possible for Him Who Believes

Some people have a hard time with faith. In Mark 9 we read the account of a perplexed father who had brought his epileptic son to the disciples and asked them to heal him. They were unsuccessful. We don't know why. Maybe it was because of the father's unbelief, or maybe it was because of the immature faith of the disciples. This distraught man now asked the living God—Jesus Christ—for help.

> "It [the epilepsy] has often thrown him into fire or water to kill him. But if you can do anything, take pity on us and help us."
> "'If you can'"? said Jesus. "Everything is possible for him who believes."
> Immediately the boy's father exclaimed, "I do believe; help me overcome my unbelief!" (Mark 9:22-24).

Jesus healed that boy *as well as* the father's weak faith. If you have a weak faith, the Bible tells us that our loving and faithful God will even help us with our doubt—just as he did with the father of the epileptic boy.

Scripture tells us that our faith needs to be childlike. We need to come to Jesus with innocence and trust. A child's basic nature is to be dependent upon and confident in his natural father. Likewise, we are to show that childlike faith toward our Father in heaven (see Psalm 22:9-10; Matthew 19:14; Mark 10:14-15). Someone once said, "Feed your faith and doubt will starve to death." The father in this story was feeding his faith in his interaction with Jesus.

One thing we learn from biblical accounts of faith is that faith is most powerful during a crisis. Both Old and New Testament saints, through their abiding faith, battled tremendous challenges to see victory. We too may suffer affliction, lose our job, have our home destroyed by a flood, experience the death of a loved one, or worse. But if we have an abiding faith in God, we know that the ultimate, eternal picture is one that God has painted.

Chuck Swindoll has often said, "Nothing touches you that hasn't first passed through the loving hands of God." If we really believe that He has our best interest in mind, these temporal problems will take their proper place on the eternal timeline. (For some inspiration, read Lamentations 3:21-24; Zephaniah 3:15; and 1 Peter 1:7.)

"The Righteous Shall Live by Faith"

In Paul's letter to the Galatians, he compares the foolishness of the law with the promises that faith holds. His basic message is that we are free in Christ and are no longer bondservants to the laws, traditions, or personal preferences of others. Because of our maturing faith, we can experience the freedom of our salvation.

A mature faith can propel people into a new world of thinking where risk and adventure are looked upon as opportunities to see God's hand at work in their lives. Such was the case with Don Stephens and a team of 175 students and volunteer crew. They were trying to ready the Anastasis—a 522-foot ocean liner owned by YWAM (Youth With A Mission)—to sail from its port at Athens, Greece on missionary trips around the world. There can be no doubt that these people believed in God's power and grace. Daily they trusted God for their very survival. Their faith encouraged others and began a revival in that land.

How did it happen? Here is part of the story of this inspiring group of faithful people, as told to Loren Cunningham, founder and president of YWAM:

"They are the heroes," Don said, bragging, as he always did about his team. His young men and women had to worm their way into the stinking bilge of the ship to clean it. They scrubbed, scoured, polished, and painted. And all of this with so little money that they could only buy generator oil for a few hours of electricity at a time. Their food was mostly peanut butter and rice and beans. The Athens port authorities would not let them live onboard, so they stayed in an old hotel that had been damaged in a recent earthquake. But just as in Hawaii we had decided not to wait on a tool (the buildings and campus) before obeying

God's call to start the university, so also Don and his team in Athens decided not to wait for their tool (the ship) before obeying God's call to a mercy ministry. At every opportunity, his teams were out helping Greek people suffering from the earthquake. They were also hard at work every day taking the Gospel onto the streets right where they were.

I was pleased. "Don," I said, "we're getting the message aren't we? God wants us to focus our attention on His call, not on His tools."

All of YWAM (Youth With A Mission) began to help in the finances needed for the ship itself. But the young people under Don and Deyon continued to be responsible for their own support, usually through regular, non-begging, informative letters to folks back home.

Very often the provision had an air of mystery about it. The kids would write to one person and get back a letter of encouragement from someone else—often someone they'd never heard of. Very often, funds too would come in from a totally unexpected direction.

The closer the Anastasis came to being seaworthy, the more often Don insisted on pulling back to basics. Why were the young people willing to crawl between the plates of the ship to clean it out? Because they were evangelists. They were already asking God for a huge harvest, thousands upon thousands more who would be helped in acts of mercy. In preparation for this releasing, Don became intrigued by the link between prayer-and-fasting, guidance, and a good harvest. Jesus, after all, began His incredibly fruitful ministry after the wilderness fast. Perhaps the ship team should do the same!

So Don and Deyon and their 175 team members began a 40-day fast, rotating commitment so that at all times several people were doing the spiritual work of fasting and praying. I was fascinated, remembering the same kind of fasting-prayer in the Dawson's New Zealand home immediately before the substantial release of workers for YWAM.

The 40-day spiritual discipline in Athens was just about over. One day the telephone rang. It was Don.

"Loren, are you ready?"

"Ready!" I could tell from the lightness in Don's voice that the news was good.

"Just make notes, good friend," Don said. "As soon as we began to see what was happening, we took very accurate account and these figures are not exaggerated by even one fish. Listen to this . . ." And then Don told the story of what happened as the crew was fasting and praying to be guided toward an abundant harvest.

One of the ship's crew was walking along the beach near the hotel where the team lived. Suddenly he saw 12 medium-sized fish jump over the rocks into a shallow tide pool right at his feet. He caught them and ran to the hotel to show the others. It was a big enough catch that a few staffers were able to have a fish fry to supplement their rice that night. A few days later, a large tuna jumped out of the sea onto the beach. This time, more YWAMers got to eat a portion with their evening meal.

Again, a few days later, one of our young team members from Dallas, Texas, was having her quiet time settled on the rocks by the sea. Suddenly fish began to jump. She whooped and shouted. Local Greek families saw what was happening and ran up to catch the fish, too. Becky gathered 210 fish and the Greek families took two or three times that much home.

But the biggest fish story was yet to come.

"Just last Tuesday, Loren, at eight in the morning, the fish began jumping again!" Don and Deyon and the others ran shouting, down to the sea. For 150 yards down shore they could see fish leaping onto land. They ran back to the hotel and grabbed every container they could find—plastic buckets, dishpans, large bags. "Our crew spent 45 minutes gathering fish as fast as we could," Don said. What was causing them to leap up on the shore that way: Nobody knew. Their Greek friends had never seen anything like it. They said, "God is with these people."

When the great fishing party was over, they counted what they had been given in the unusual way. "Loren, you won't believe how many!" Don said. "There were 8,301—over one ton of fish, Loren! You can imagine the praise session we had right there on the beach. This was the encouragement we needed that the ministry of the Anastasis is going to be very, very special indeed."

Just as suddenly as the fish began to jump, signaling an abundant harvest for the Anastasis's mercy ministry, so was the final money released to pay for the technical work being done by the shipyard.[2]

There is no doubt that because of the faithful work of a few, many were blessed. God poured out His grace upon a shipload of people who were willing to be obedient in faith.

Will God always fill our boats with a ton of fish if we trust Him? Not necessarily. His plans and ways are unknown to humankind. Is He *able* to fill our boats with an abundant harvest? Most definitely. If we are faithful followers, God delights in surprising us with His wonderful blessings.

With the same faith that led Lowell to tie on that lure and make just one more cast, we can place faith in God and receive blessings from His hands. Friend, Jesus is asking you to tie on the first lure and make that cast of faith into an eternal relationship with the living God. Do it today—a special catch is awaiting you!

The Journey Begins Here

God wants a personal relationship with each one of us. To have that relationship, God asks that we believe in Him and His only begotten son, who died on Calvary's cross that we might have eternal life. To take that first step of faith—to receive Him as Lord and Savior—Scripture provides these instructions:

1. Admit to God that you are a sinner and are in need of a Savior (Romans 3:23).

2. Be willing to repent (turn away from) your sins (Acts 3:19).

3. Believe that Jesus Christ died for you on the cross and rose bodily from the grave (1 Corinthians 15:1-8).

4. By prayer, with an attitude of faith, invite Jesus Christ to come in and take control of your life through the Holy Spirit.

5. Following your salvation experience, you need to get into a "fishermen's fellowship" (a church).

6. Acknowledge your decision publicly. Tell others of your newfound faith.

Personal Growth

• What does it mean to have faith? (Read Hebrews 11:1 for some insights.)

• What things do you accept by faith?

• Have you accepted God's forgiveness of your sins by faith?

PERSONAL PROFILE

Lowell Lundstrom

Background—Born in Minneapolis, Minnesota. Raised in South Dakota.

Age When First Fish Caught—Five years old (caught a fish at Lake Itaska in Northern Minnesota).

Favorite Bible Verses—Psalm 34:6 and John 3:30.

Family—Married to Connie for 40 years. Four children (two boys, two girls), two grandchildren.

Favorite Fishing Hole—Big Sandy Lake in North Minaki, Ontario, Canada.

Favorite Fishing Lure—Shad Rap or Daredevil.

Preferred Equipment—Spinning.

Most Respected Fishing Pro/Mentor or Instructor—Al and Ron Lindner.

Personal Comments—"Immediately after receiving Christ, I stood up and said, 'Wait until my friends hear about this!' I haven't stopped telling them, and over 500,000 people have come to the Lord through the Lowell Lundstrom Crusades. Praise God."

One of Lowell's favorite things to tell new believers is this:

> Give your heart to Jesus,
> Try Him for six months.
> If you don't like how things are going,
> You get all your sins back.

7

Living Without Anxiety

Fishing with Jim Grassi and John Merritt

My eyes popped open as I realized that my hunting and fishing buddy John Merritt, senior pastor of a very large suburban church, was beginning to prepare for the day's activities. The other six voyagers with us were still in dreamland.

John and I crept out onto the slippery deck to see how our crab pots fared during the night. We had set three of them around the 45-foot yacht along with two halibut rods.

John slipped over the side onto the zodiak and started pulling in each crab pot. Suddenly, my halibut rod starting dancing on the rail with the drag beginning to peel off the big Penn reel. I grabbed the rod and set the hook with a vengeance. No alarm clock was needed to awaken the entire boat. Our yelling stirred everyone's curiosity.

After John finished pulling his thirty-first keeper crab on board, the skipper was gaffing (or spearing) my 35-pound halibut. What a way to start the day! The captain pulled up anchor as we motored in a southerly direction through the infamous Icy Straits along the inland passage that separates British Columbia from the offshore islands.

This picturesque waterway was incredibly beautiful as the majestic glaciers and steep mountains cascaded into the canal. The stark contrast between the snowcapped purple mountains and the bright blue skies was almost surrealistic. Many large cruise boats use this waterway as a sightseeing route because of its scenic beauty and abundant wildlife. One can typically see eagles, bears, deer, salmon, and a variety of whales, including a few killer whales.

We spent most of the day crossing the eyes of halibut with a little time spent trolling for salmon. As we motored into a docking area that evening, John suggested that we take off and return to the cove where we had spent the first night. He wanted to check out the area for any silver salmon and do some exploring for black bears.

John and I had already spent ten days together on a caribou hunt. We had limited success and a number of "close encounters" with the weather, floatplanes, and pilots who forgot to pick us up. This part of our trip was supposed to be the relaxing phase.

Recognizing the lateness of the hour, I was content to stay onboard and help the others clean the halibut. John, however, was passionate—you might even say impetuous—and insisted that we scout out the cove. He headed for the cabin to get his hunting gear. I decided it wasn't a good idea to let my partner proceed without some backup, so I grabbed some of my survival gear and a rifle and jumped into the small inflatable raft with John. We headed northeast, carefully noting our course and counting each channel between the multiple islands scattered throughout the area.

We motored for more than an hour before we finally saw the infamous cove. After securing the raft, we made our way to a spawning stream to see if the salmon had resumed their activities. We were also on the watch for black bears.

John and I agreed that we could only spend an hour on this trek before we needed to make our way back to the yacht. What we hadn't counted on was the speed of the incoming tide which had now totally filled the small bay where we had beached our boat. Fortunately, we had placed an anchor overboard before leaving the raft, which saved it from being washed away.

After a time, we waded out to the raft, climbed aboard, and secured our gear as we turned to the south to head back. The steep slopes on the west side of the gorge separated us from the embracing light of the setting sun. The dark shadows of the mountains presented an eerie invitation to investigate each inlet for a shortcut back to the safety and security of our mother vessel.

At first it seemed like an adventure. But as the minutes ticked by, it soon became a struggle for survival. The cold night air and freezing mist from the wake of our boat reminded us of the reality that if our small boat capsized, we would only be able to survive about three minutes before hypothermia set in.

As we ducked in and out of coves, it became apparent that the "secret passageway" that was so easily recognizable in the daytime was carefully hidden with a curtain of darkness and mystery. The water was now 10 to 15 feet deeper than when we started. Islands previously used as reference points were now several feet underwater.

Our choices were limited. We could continue to search in and out of darkened coves, risking the possibility of puncturing our inflatable boat on a submerged jagged rock. Or we could venture out into the deep channel a half mile from shore and motor along with the killer whales who were periodically surfacing.

The audible prayers of two outdoorsmen filled the night air with hope and expectation. John was apologizing for being impetuous. I was apologizing for taking an extra ten minutes to check out one more stream.

The wind and waves began to increase as we continued our course south. We both felt that once we got around the large island, we would find our way back to the ship. The skipper had moored our boat in an isolated cove off the Icy Straits where we had been fishing most of the day.

Would we have enough gas to get around the point? Would the wind be greater once we turned to the west? Would the boat still be there, or had our comrades left to try and find us? All sorts of questions began to cross our minds.

The drive toward the point seemed like an eternity. Darkness was everywhere since the moon had yet to appear. The constant groan of the engine suddenly stopped. Now we were adrift in the middle of the channel.

John's eyes looked like saucers. My heart raced as I imagined the headlines in tomorrow's newspaper: "Two Bay Area Clergymen Swallowed by Whales." We both grabbed for the gas tank with the hope that the vent cap had vibrated shut thereby cutting off the air supply to the tank. Sure enough— that was exactly what had happened. After a few pulls of the starting rope, we both sighed with relief as the motor once again began to putt and roar.

Fear and trepidation filled the air as the wind and waves continued to increase. Distress became our companion as we turned the corner into the windy sea. The raft began to buckle under our feet as the waves and swells banged against the fragile hull.

A faint light appeared out across the horizon. It was a light from a nearby boat that could possibly direct us to safety. The decision whether to move further away from shore to reach the boat or to keep moving around the point toward what might be our mooring site was not an easy one to make.

I convinced John that our best chance for a rescue, and for a confirmation of our position, was to head for that boat. After several minutes we intercepted it as it was making its way toward a rendezvous with a trolling ship several miles from our location.

The crew was huddled around a heater sipping on warm coffee in the wheelhouse. They peered out the fogged window to see two guys with guns dressed in camouflage gear waving fanatically for them to stop. They wanted no part of dealing with us. Apparently a group of modern-day pirates had pulled off a robbery on the high seas a few nights before. Most of these transport tugs carried large quantities of cash which they used to purchase fish from trolling vessels. They were a transport service for the fishing fleet.

It wasn't until we yelled, "Please help us!" that they were convinced we were indeed lost and frightened. Perhaps it was the look of fear on our faces—or maybe the fact that no robbers in their right minds would attempt to commit a crime in an eight-foot inflatable raft with a ten-horsepower engine—that caused them to stop.

The skipper opened his cabin door and yelled, "What in the _____ are you doing at this time of night in that little boat?" He elaborated on our mothers' lack of wisdom for even birthing two stupid individuals like us, and then proceeded to give us a short course on seamanship. After we had been sufficiently humbled, he advised us that the mooring area we were looking for was indeed just around the corner.

As we putted into the dock, our colleagues came out onto the deck. They looked at us like we were either the two most lucky idiots in the world or that we were the greatest outdoorsmen and skilled seamen they had ever seen.

Our casual attitude and lack of hysteria seemed to calm their fears that they had two lunatics on their hands. We composed ourselves enough to eat what remained of dinner and retired to the stateroom we shared.

I don't know if it was our ecstatic laughter or the fact that we kept everyone awake most of the night talking about our adventure, but by dawn everyone was quite convinced that we should be separated from the rest of the fishermen. John and I spent the rest of the trip fishing off the bow of the ship. The inflatable raft was stored and locked on the top deck, and our captain broke out the shackles just in case.

"I Will Fear No Evil"

As we relived this adventure, John and I thought a great deal about being impetuous and fearful. Far from being a problem limited to neurotics, fear undermines the spiritual vigor of many Christians, and dampens their witness and worship of the Lord. *Anxiety is a joy-robber.*

On March 4, 1933, Franklin D. Roosevelt, during his inaugural address, said, "The only thing we have to fear is fear itself." This might have been a great way to rally the nation, but the reality is that *we all* have fearful times. The increase of crime and violence in our schools and neighborhoods daily threatens our young people. Stories of terrorism and bombings fill our newspapers and cause the most optimistic among us to be fearful. The threat of nuclear annihilation from a Third World lunatic has the whole country concerned. The alarming spread of disease—especially AIDS—creates tremors in every community.

Lloyd Ogilvie, in his book *Twelve Steps to Living Without Fear*, notes that "fear has reached epidemic proportions in America. It is contagious. We become infected with it and pass it on to others. Like a disease, fear saps our energy and robs us of joy in life. It cripples many Christians and often pervades our families, even our churches."[1]

There will always be things that cause fear in our lives. Marshall Nay, one of Napoleon's commanders, was a frail man but a gallant warrior. Often before a battle his knees shook so much that he had a hard time staying upright on his horse. He would literally strap his shoulders down. On one occasion his knees trembled so badly that he yelled out, "Shake will you, shake will you, if you knew where I was going to take you this day you'd really shake!"

Faith Dispels Fear

The Bible has much to say about fear. The heartening challenge, "Fear not," appears some 366 times in Scripture. In each case the challenge is followed by an assurance that God will protect His people and redeem them from their anxieties.

Either God's Word is totally true or it isn't. When God directs us 366 times to "Fear not," we either trust and obey Him, or we allow our frightened thoughts to dominate our lives. We either believe He is fully capable of providing peace and comfort to get us through the struggle, or that His grace and might isn't sufficient.

The apostle Paul instructs us, "Do not be anxious about anything, but in everything, by prayer and petition, with thanksgiving, present your requests to God. And the peace of God, which transcends all understanding, will guard your hearts and your minds in Christ Jesus" (Philippians 4:6-7). Simply put—*worry about nothing, but pray about everything*.

Paul also tells us to get our minds off our circumstances and our panic so that we can place our focus on Him who is able: "Finally, brothers, whatever is true, whatever is noble, whatever is right, whatever is pure, whatever is lovely, whatever is admirable—if anything is excellent or praiseworthy—think about such things. Whatever you have learned or received or heard from me, or seen in me—put it into practice. And the God of peace will be with you" (Philippians 4:8-9).

What do you think about when fear is upon you? According to Paul, we should focus our minds on things that are pure, lovely, and admirable—*positive* things. The mind cannot focus upon two things at once. The minute John and I focused upon the cold dark night and the near-hopeless plight of our situation, the alarm of apprehension filled our boat. As we shifted our thoughts to God's promises, and set our confidence in the guidance He was giving, the peace of God began to flood the raft.

What are the things that cause you to worry? Can you surrender them to God and focus upon the peace that "transcends all understanding"? You say, "Jim, you don't know what I'm going through and how tough it is to give up my fear!" You're right, I don't know the specifics. But I too struggle with fear and anxiety. I *do* know that God can handle all your distress, if you only place each problem into His warm, loving hands (Psalm 34:9).

As the apostle Peter put it, "Cast all your anxiety on him because he cares for you" (1 Peter 5:7). Remember, Peter was the ultimate fisherman of his day and he constantly wrestled with his faith and obedience. He was often fearful as he faced threatening circumstances. Yet, at the end of his ministry, he had learned how to cope with his fear—*casting* all anxiety at the feet of Jesus.

There's a lesson we can learn from the fine art of casting: *The longer the rod, the longer the cast.* A distance caster will not select a five-foot rod to throw a three-quarter-ounce casting plug. He will select an eight- to nine-foot rod so he can really fling the cast and get the maximum distance between himself and the casting plug.

Faith is a lot like that casting rod. The greater our faith (the longer the rod), the more distance we can get between ourselves and our problems. When we, by faith, cast our anxieties upon the Father, He wants us to flee from them and trust Him to deal with them.

For me, this is where the rubber meets the road. I can go through the motions of giving my fears to God and then, moments later, take them right back when I get up from my knees. Satan loves to disturb our minds and create doubt about God's ability to take control. We must give our fears to God and, by faith, keep them there.

The disciples learned this important lesson too. They had just finished listening to Jesus teach the parables of faith regarding the Sower and the Soils and the Mustard Seed. They had witnessed His miracles and sat at His feet to learn of His ways. Their faith should have been strong. However, their weak faith surfaced as they found themselves face to face with an angry sea.

That day when evening came, he said to his disciples, "Let us go over to the other side." Leaving the crowd behind, they took him along, just as he was, in the boat. There were also other boats with him. A furious squall came up, and the waves broke over the boat, so that it was nearly swamped. Jesus was in the stern, sleeping on a cushion. The disciples woke him and said to him, "Teacher, don't you care if we drown?"

He got up, rebuked the wind and said to the waves, "Quiet! Be still!" Then the wind died down and it was completely calm.

He said to his disciples, "Why are you so afraid? Do you still have no faith?"

They were terrified and asked each other, "Who is this? Even the wind and the waves obey him!" (Mark 4:35-41).

These seasoned fishermen-sailors were very familiar with the Sea of Galilee and its capricious nature. Their futile struggle against the overwhelming sea and wind was indicative of the level of faith they had at that point in their spiritual development. They wanted to handle their fear with their own resources and strength. It was only when things seemed totally out of control that they reached out to their Savior.

How often we use the same approach when confronted with struggles! I'm embarrassed to admit that John and I first focused all our attention on how we could save ourselves in our seemingly hopeless situation. Our first reaction should have been to ask for God's help. How slow we are to learn.

Rx for Fear

What is the prescription for fear? Though an entire book could be written on this, in what follows are some key principles that have helped me.

First, when we focus on the *peace of Jesus* we can see that things aren't as bad as they could be. When Jesus is in the midst of a situation, we can rest in Him. Our Savior modeled a peaceful, even restful, attitude to the disciples as He slept in the stern on a cushion. If we are truly His, we should be comforted in the knowledge that nothing can touch us that hasn't first gone through the sovereign hands of God. As Thomas Kelly put it, "We can have an altar of peace no matter what is going on around us, if we go to Jesus who will give a special peace."[2]

Many people like me, who are hands-on managers, have been successful because of our God given-abilities and leadership style. But, of all people, we must remember the wisdom of relinquishing control to the ultimate manager— God. I remember reading somewhere,

> *Don't feel totally, personally, irrevocably, eternally responsible for everything. That's my job.*
> —GOD

A second principle that can help us cope with fear involves recognizing the *presence of Jesus*. Let me illustrate it this way: When President Nixon was at the pinnacle of his power, Chuck Colson and Henry Kissinger were accompanying him to a meeting on Air Force One on a very stormy evening. The plane was literally bounced around the sky. Colson and Kissinger became concerned. In fact, Kissinger leaned over to Colson and said, "I'm sure glad the president's on this plane." But Nixon was not Jesus. Having faith in the saving power of a president is not going to help any of us. Our faith needs to rest in the recognition that Jesus is present in our lives.

The disciples had failed to remember that Jesus was in the boat. When Jesus is in *our* boat, we need not fret. He is ever-present in the life of the believer. He is never separated from us. Paul reminds us of this principle in Romans 8:38: "For I am convinced that neither death nor life, neither angels nor demons, neither the present nor the future, nor any powers, either height nor depth, nor anything else in all creation, will be able to separate us from the love of God that is in Christ Jesus our Lord."

A third principle involves a recognition of the *power of Jesus*. Apparently the frightened disciples forgot that Jesus was God-incarnate and that all the power in the universe was and is directed by Him. So, in their fear, they woke Him. "He got up, rebuked the wind and said to the waves, 'Quiet! Be still!' Then the wind died down and it was completely calm" (Mark 4:39). We might paraphrase what Jesus said this way: "Stormy sea, at ease! Now!" Wow—what power!

The disciples had previously seen Jesus heal people, cast out demons, change water into wine, and perform many wondrous miracles. Yet, apparently, they couldn't trust His sovereign control of nature while on the Sea of Galilee.

It's all too easy to say, "If I would have been one of those disciples and seen all of Jesus' miracles, I would have trusted Him in that situation." Before we become too cynical over their lack of faith, however, let me ask, when was the last time *you* became panicked? Personally, I can tell you that I'm no different from the disciples. God has richly blessed me and my family. He has shown His power of healing to each of us in dramatic fashion. He has calmed the "seas of fear" when my ministry seemed to be on the verge of sinking. God's power and protection have been evident over and over again. *But how often I forget about His miracles!* Too often, in my initial fear, I forget about the real power I can appropriate by calling upon the strength of God to help me ride out the storm. This is what happened on those icy waters in Alaska. John and I forgot about the power of Jesus, and foolishly tried to rely on our own skill and wisdom.

A fourth principle for coping with fear involves recognizing the *personality of Jesus*. On the boat, Jesus showed that He cared for His disciples. He didn't turn over and ignore them but rather met them at their point of greatest need. This same Jesus is here to love and encourage us. His personality is that of a gracious and kind servant who really cares for His creation. If He cares enough for sparrows and the lilies of the field, don't you think He cares for you too (see Matthew 6:25-34)?

You can give *all* your fears and anxieties to Jesus.

Personal Growth

- Do you have a support group that can help you during fearful times (Ecclesiastes 4:9)? How might you utilize those individuals along with God's Word to battle frightening feelings?

- What are some positive, faith-building thoughts you can reflect on when discouragement and worry cross your path?

- When fear strikes—remember, "the battle is not yours, but God's" (2 Chronicles 20:15).

PERSONAL PROFILE

Jim Grassi

Background—Born and raised in Oakland, California. Executive Director of Let's Go Fishing Ministries. Popular author/ TV co-host, and conference speaker. Former tournament professional fisherman who has taught fishing to more than one million people through classes, seminars, and sports show appearances. An ordained minister and recipient of the "Faith and Freedom Award." Thoroughly enjoys all kinds of fishing—especially with his twin sons and grandchild.

Age When First Fish Caught—Five years old.

Favorite Bible Verses—Matthew 4:19, 1 Corinthians 10:13, and Deuteronomy 6:4-9.

Family—Wife, Louise, and twin sons.

Favorite Fishing Hole—Lake Shasta, California.

Favorite Fishing Lure—Surface Plugs; Spinner Baits.

Preferred Equipment—Bait Casting–Ultra Light.

Most Respected Fishing Pro/Mentor or Instructor—the late Elmer Etter (father-in-law).

Personal Comments—"My greatest desire is to hear those encouraging words from my heavenly Father, 'Well done, my good servant'" (Luke 19:17).

PERSONAL PROFILE

John Merritt

Background—Grew up in the Midwest as the oldest of five children. His father was a pastor and outdoorsman who taught him a lot about God, fishing, and hunting. John presently serves as senior pastor of Crosswinds Church in Dublin, California (one of the largest seeker-sensitive churches in the Bay Area). He is a well-respected speaker with a heart for overseas missions.

Age When First Fish Caught—Five years old.

Favorite Bible Verse—Psalm 19:14.

Family—Wife, Debbie, and three children.

Favorite Fishing Hole—San Francisco Bay and the ocean.

Favorite Fishing Lure—Rapala.

Preferred Equipment—Ultra Light Spinning.

Most Respected Fishing Pro/Mentor or Instructor—Al Lindner—In-Fisherman Network.

Personal Comments—"I really appreciate my Christian heritage."

8

Joy-Filled Living

Fishing with Jimmy Houston

ach Saturday morning, for more than two decades,
dedicated sportsmen have gathered around their
television sets to watch their favorite fishing show
host, Jimmy Houston, on ESPN. His wit and wisdom have
entertained and challenged many aspiring anglers. Some
would say he is the best fisherman in the world. Many have
attested to his outstanding casting skills.

Others might commend Jimmy for his entrepreneurship
and ability to attract sponsors. Outdoor writer John Phillips
describes him as having "the personality of a circus clown,
the energy of a ping-pong ball, the business mind of Donald
Trump, and the compassion of your neighborhood minister."
That's the Jimmy I know and love!

We've been friends for more than 17 years now. It was
my pleasure to have worked with Jimmy as one of my board
members while I served as executive director of the Fellowship of Christian Anglers Society (FOCAS). We've filmed
five television programs together, including a few while
fishing on the Sea of Galilee. I've viewed him closely under
all kinds of pressure and circumstances. He is a remarkable

icon who continues to inspire me with his honesty and passion.

Joy is a key component of Jimmy's personality. When God gave out the "joy juice," Jimmy was first in line and received an ample supply of that blessing. In fact, the first quality I think of when I hear Jimmy's name, or see that Cheshire cat grin underneath his shaggy blond hair, is a child of God who has good cheer.

When I asked Jimmy to share his all-time favorite fishing story, it was no surprise that he didn't tell me about one of his personal exploits but rather dealt with the time he took his daughter along on a filming trip to Cato Creek Lake in Texas. Sherry had just turned 12 years old and was anxious to prove herself worthy of following in the footsteps of her champion fisherwoman mother, Chris. Chris has won virtually every honor and tournament on the Ladies Bass circuit. She is the circuit's all-time money winner, and has the respect and admiration of fisherman everywhere.

As with most self-assured youth, Sherry didn't listen to dad regarding her choice of bait. Despite the fact that the cameras were rolling and Jimmy was already working on his second limit,* Sherry held firm on wanting to throw her favorite white spinnerbait. "White is right!" she shouted to Jimmy.

The old pro just kept smiling and chucking his blue and chartreuse single-blade Strike King spinnerbait, waiting to catch another fish and prove his daughter wrong— *again*. Suddenly, Sherry screamed, "Daddy, I've got a big 'un! I mean really big!"

Jimmy wasn't too excited until he saw the spunky bass shoot out of the water like a Polaris missile. This wasn't just any fish. It was a trophy largemouth bass that was giving Sherry a lesson in patience and perseverance. The screams

---

*A "limit" is the maximum quantity of fish that may be taken legally in a specified period.

from Sherry and shouts of encouragement from Dad filled the cove with excitement. Sherry was afraid she might lose her first trophy bass.

The drag peeled out the stretched line, and her confidence began to grow. As the fat seven-pound bass approached the boat, Jimmy reached over and scooped it out by the lower jaw. The pride and excitement written all over his face said it all.

A Joyful Heart

As Jimmy recalled this wonderful story, I could sense the genuine joy in his heart. It is a joy that comes from a life filled with family and Jesus Christ. One would almost think that Jimmy and his family have never known hardship. The truth is, however, that the strangling stresses of an evil society have occasionally gripped his family, challenging their faith and threatening their happiness.

I remember a time when Jimmy was constantly being harassed by an unfriendly company. The company did all kinds of things that potentially could have robbed Jimmy of his joy and confidence. This stressful situation went on for years. Yet Jimmy's heart never became faint as he continued to live a spirit-filled life before all those who came into contact with him.

Samuel Shoemaker once said, "The surest mark of a Christian is not faith, or even love, but joy." Jimmy's joy comes from knowing Jesus Christ as his personal Savior. His life is a vibrant testimony to the fact that joy is dependent upon Jesus, not upon the journey. Despite the trials he has encountered, he has always chosen to focus upon the positive aspects of his life and faith. Jimmy is a living illustration of an "attitude of gratitude."

His positive outlook reminds me of a story of two boys who were given a test by a psychologist. One boy was rich and spoiled because everything had always been given to him, although he was still not happy. Knowing the rich boy's appreciation for the outdoors, the doctor placed him in a room filled with guns, bows, bass boats, and all the fishing gear one could imagine.

The psychologist took the other boy—a destitute young man who nevertheless had a positive outlook on life—and placed him at a dingy pond at the end of a sewage treatment plant. He gave him an old broken rod and reel with one lure tied on the frayed line.

Several hours passed. The doctor then went to the room where he had left the rich child, only to find him laying on the floor in tears because he was so bored.

He then went to the poor boy at the pond only to find him singing with joy. He was running up and down the bank, casting and shouting, "Where are you, Mr. Fish?" The doctor asked the boy what he was doing. The boy explained, "With all this cover and murky water, there must be a trophy bass in here somewhere!"

What is joy? Jimmy Houston would tell you it's an attitude characterized by a feeling of pure satisfaction, pleasure, and fulfillment. From a biblical perspective, it is contentment and calmness that results from a strong and abiding faith in the power and grace of the Almighty.

> Joy is prayer—Joy is strength—Joy is love—Joy is a net of love by which you can catch souls. . . . The best way to show our gratitude to God and to people is to accept everything with joy. A joyful heart is the inevitable result of a heart burning with love. Never let anything so fill you with sorrow as to make you forget the joy of the Christ risen.[1]

The word *joy* appears some 218 times in the Bible. Joy goes hand in hand with faith. As you read these various verses, it becomes clear that joy is a deep inner peace based on faith that projects a sense of great well-being and confidence.

Happiness, on the other hand, is more dependent on our circumstances. We feel happy when the job promotion comes in on time. We feel cheerful when our financial dreams are met. We are glad when our favorite team wins a game, and especially happy when they go to the Super Bowl. But these feelings last only until the next trial or failure occurs. With happiness, there is no enduring significance to any event or material possession. Joy, by contrast, is not dependent on circumstances. No matter what comes our way, we can have joy because we are walking with Jesus.

A joyful spirit has always given Jimmy Houston the competitive edge in the fishing and casting tournaments in which he has participated. More importantly, joy has given him a philosophy for living. What is *your* approach to life?

Joy Is Foundational to Our Faith

It is natural for us to focus on the trials and struggles of daily life. For most of us, the pressures of our stress-filled environment create demands that rip and tear at our character and spirit. For those of us with sensitive, caring natures, the critics and scoffers can pilfer moments of joy from our lives. Worry, fear, temptation, anger, and unresolved conflict are like thieves in the night that take every opportunity to steal away our delight.

Certainly there was a great deal of pressure on the first-century disciples. The serious nature of their calling and fate was etched into their minds every time Jesus chiseled away at their character.

As Jesus broke bread with them during the celebration of His last Feast of the Passover, He impressed upon them that "His hour had come" (*see* John 12:27). He described His fate (the cross) and continued to teach them important lessons about leadership, serving, sacrifice, and obedience. After imploring them to abide in His love, He said: "These things

I have spoken to you, that My joy may be in you, and that your joy may be made full" (John 15:11).

Jesus wanted to see His joy remain in the disciples, fill them, and totally consume them. Part of that process involves bearing fruit. If disciples bear fruit and continue in their love of Jesus, they will rejoice. Fruitful and faithful disciples are joyful servants. Christ's love provides a continual feast to fill their hungry souls. "They feast on the abundance of your house; you give them drink from your river of delights" (Psalm 36:8).

Jesus tells us to "seek first His kingdom and His righteousness; and all these things shall be added to you" (Matthew 6:33). What things will be added? Among other things, the fruit of the spirit, which includes "love, *joy*, peace, patience, kindness, goodness, faithfulness, gentleness, self-control; against such things there is no law" (Galatians 5:22).

On a recent book tour across the country, I was doing a live one-hour television program on the Cornerstone Network in Pittsburgh. Throughout the program, the host asked the viewing audience to call if they had any prayer needs. After the program, a volunteer delivered a one-inch thick stack of individual requests and concerns, many of which dealt with life and death issues.

I started to think about the many trials Christians face and why we should be joyful. Certainly many of the viewers were not particularly joyful about their circumstances. What promise could we pass on to them?

I believe it comes down to this: If our hearts and minds are set on eternal issues, then our joy comes from knowing that the foundation of our faith is secure, no matter what circumstances come our way. Joy comes from knowing our eternal destiny, and that our time on earth is like a drop of water in a huge lake. The real issue has to do with where we will spend eternity. If we have accepted Jesus Christ as our personal Savior, we have the guarantee of eternal life. The temporary struggles and pain we experience are just that—*temporary*.

Joy also comes in knowing we have the ultimate companion and friend who will never leave us or forsake us. The Holy Spirit is our comforter and guide. He is never capricious or unfaithful (John 14:16,26). In difficult times, He provides the inner peace that is required to maintain a deep and abiding joy.

We also receive encouragement and joy in the knowledge that friends and relatives who know Christ will be with us forever (1 Thessalonians 4:13-17). There will be no more painful good-byes, no more funerals, and no loved ones moving away from home. The assurance that the kingdom of heaven is at hand for all who believe (Matthew 10:7) is a promise to be claimed and secured with joy.

People who know Jimmy Houston are amazed at his mental toughness, his competitive strength, and capability. *It's all rooted in his joy!* Without joy, the Christian faith cannot maintain its power. One thing that separates Christianity from other religious experiences is the Christian's ability to draw strength from inner joy. As the prophet Nehemiah put it, "The joy of the Lord is my strength" (Nehemiah 8:10).

Joy in the Midst of Trials

Throughout the writings of the apostle Paul, we are continually impressed with the magnitude of his suffering. Trial after trial, we witness his faith tested, his body tortured, and his character assassinated (2 Corinthians 4:8-10). *We also see his joy.* Some 31 times Paul talks about joy in his writings. One example of this is found in Philippians, where he begins and ends a crucial passage with a comment on joy:

> But what does it matter? The important thing is that in every way, whether from false motives or true, Christ is preached. And because of this I *rejoice*. Yes, and I will continue to *rejoice*, for I know that through

your prayers and the help given by the Spirit of Jesus Christ, what has happened to me will turn out for my deliverance. I eagerly expect and hope that I will in no way be ashamed, but will have sufficient courage so that now as always Christ will be exalted in my body, whether by life or by death. For to me, to live is Christ and to die is gain. If I am to go on living in the body, this will mean fruitful labor for me. Yet what shall I choose? I do not know! I am torn between the two: I desire to depart and be with Christ, which is better by far; but it is more necessary for you that I remain in the body. Convinced of this, I know that I will remain, and I will continue with all of you for your progress and joy in the faith, so that through my being with you again your *joy* in Christ Jesus will overflow on account of me (Philippians 1:18-26, emphasis added).

Paul knew there would be trials, disappointments, threats, pain, and suffering. No Christian is exempt from the testings of life. However, it is because we persevere and become approved that we will receive the crown of life (James 1:12). This, my friend, is why James could agree with Paul's teaching and say, "Consider it all joy, my brethren, when you encounter various trials" (verse 2).

To help remind Jimmy of God's faithfulness, his wife Chris has embroidered on the back of each of his tournament fishing shirts, "Rejoice in the Lord always" (Philippians 4:4). When Jimmy has had a particularly bad tournament, she hangs the shirt on the rearview mirror so Jimmy will see it when he gets into the van for the long trip home.

Are you denying or avoiding painful trials? Don't avoid them, for they will refine your faith, and this will ultimately increase your joy. Remember, joy is refined and perfected in the crucible of trials.

Joy in the Midst of Suffering

Sheldon Kopp once said, "Life can be counted on to provide all the pain that any of us might need."[2] My friend Tim Hanzel is a living example of a victorious Christian who daily struggles with the overwhelming pain and torment of a body that was broken and crushed in a mountain climbing accident.

Tim was an all-American athlete at Stanford University and he went on to found the Summit Expedition Ministry. His athleticism and climbing abilities enabled him to accomplish feats that most outdoorsmen could only dream about.

It was just one little slip on an icy path that caused a 50-foot fall that broke several bones in Tim's body and crushed his back. Despite his pain and suffering, he has determined to fight through all the anguish and misery in order to encourage others who are suffering. In his insightful book *You Gotta Keep Dancin'*, Tim encourages us to stay joyful: "If you can't change the circumstances, change the way you respond to them. God reminded me again and again that I cannot choose to be strong, but I can choose to be joyful. And when I am willing to do that, strength will follow."[3] We must remember that "pain is inevitable, but misery is optional.... Joy is simple (not to be confused with easy). At any moment in life we have at least two options, and one of them is to choose an attitude of gratitude, a posture of grace, a commitment of joy."[4]

To focus on joy when undergoing trials is a matter of concentration. We can see in the apostle Paul's life that it is a matter of fixation—and the target of focus is the Lord Jesus. Just as concentration is a characteristic of a good fisherman, so it is the key to being a joyful disciple. It is also the passport to victorious living. If our focus is fixed upon our painful circumstances, then it will be difficult to have a joyful heart. But if our attitude is one of gratitude and joy, then our outlook will be positive and enriching.

Joy Encourages Risks

People who live with fear or despair tend to lock themselves into the known and predictable. Their lives can become stale and depressed without a fresh sense of excitement and vision.

Paul encourages the believers of Philippi to be bold—to look beyond their circumstances with an expectant heart, just as *he* had an expectant heart: "I eagerly expect and hope that I will in no way be ashamed, but will have sufficient courage so that now as always Christ will be exalted in my body, whether by life or by death" (Philippians 1:20).

Are you taking any risks today? Can you see the potential for joy when you stretch your faith?

I can guarantee you that Jimmy Houston takes risks every day. He is out-front on the firing lines of life, willing to deal with the bullets and the pain. And in the midst of it all, there is joy, joy, joy!

Joy and Sacrifice

Like every other tournament fisherman, Jimmy Houston loses more tournaments than he wins. I've been with him on several occasions when he didn't perform to his capabilities or his strategy was flawed. Despite his low standing at the end of the day, I knew I could always count on his spirit to be positive and energetic.

Jimmy has truly discovered the secret of a joyful Christian life. Like the psalmist, Jimmy believes we must "be glad in the Lord and rejoice you righteous ones, and shout for joy all you who are upright in heart" (Psalm 32:11 NASB).

Most anglers who have had a difficult tournament become embarrassed and frustrated. They typically creep off to the nearest bar or lonely motel room to sulk in their despair. Jimmy, however, chooses to make himself available to his numerous fans, especially the kids. And this seems to increase his joy with each and every contact. His smile and humorous self-criticism seems to take away his frustration and inspire the crowd of onlookers.

Simple as it may seem, people who are joyful have learned to appreciate the little things in life, and there are many to choose from. Positive people tend to focus on the possibilities of tomorrow rather than the defeats of today. I'm reminded of a sign that hangs proudly at a little fishing lodge on Lake Seminole in Georgia. It is meant to inspire and encourage anglers as they come and go. As you enter the property, the sign reads, "They tore 'em up yesterday." When you drive out, you see on the backside of the sign, "Cuz, I guarantee they'll bite tomorrow."

Are you looking to a positive future? Can you experience joy today, knowing that God's desire is to provide you a "good bite" tomorrow?

As I observe Jimmy and reflect on what Scripture tells us about joy, I've gleaned ten fundamental truths that have helped me experience a more joyful life. Perhaps they'll help you too!

1. Don't take yourself so seriously—nobody else does.

2. Givers are more joyful than takers.

3. Enjoy all the little things of life—the big things should surprise you.

4. Recognize that a Christian's ultimate joy comes from knowing he or she is a child of the King. And remember, we are assured of eternal life without pain, suffering, and despair.

5. Joy does not depend on circumstances that fluctuate from day to day.

6. Joy is a deep inner peace that transcends temporary feelings of happiness.

7. Joy comes from Jesus, not from our journey in life.

8. Joy is experienced in the fullest when you take risks and stretch your faith.

9. Don't let worry or fear steal away even a moment of your joy.

10. There is a natural joy that comes from knowing the final chapter of the book—*we are His.*

Personal Growth

• Is joy the hallmark of your faith?

• What do the following verses say to you regarding the importance of joy:

> Nehemiah 8:10
>
> Psalm 43:4
>
> John 15:11
>
> John 16:20
>
> Philippians 2:2
>
> James 1:2

• Are you having a "pity party"? Think about the apostle Paul's life (2 Corinthians 4:5-10). Then reflect upon your problems. Paul encourages us to remain joyful despite our burdens. For encouragement, read 2 Corinthians 11:23-28.

• Do you detect the fruit of the Spirit in your life (Galatians 5:22)?

PERSONAL PROFILE

Jimmy Houston

Background—Raised in Oklahoma where he married his childhood sweetheart, Chris. Former insurance salesman who became a champion bass fisherman. Qualified 14 times for the Bassmasters Classic. Twice won Angler of the Year. Twenty years the host of an award-winning television program, *Jimmy Houston Outdoors*.

Age When First Fish Caught—Two or three years old.

Favorite Bible Verse—Philippians 4:4.

Family—Wife, Chris (World Champion Fisherwoman), and two children.

Favorite Fishing Hole—Lake Tenkiller, Oklahoma.

Favorite Fishing Lure—Strike King Jimmy Houston Model-Blue/Chart. Spinnerbait.

Preferred Equipment—Bait Casting 5-foot, 6-inch Shimano.

Most Respected Fishing Pro/Mentor or Instructor—Chris Houston, Larry Nixon, and Roland Martin.

Personal Comments—"As for me and my house, we will serve the Lord" (Joshua 24:15).

9

Conquering Temptation

Fishing with Homer Circle

Most anglers would agree that in terms of legendary personalities associated with the sport of fishing, one name stands out above all others—Uncle Homer.

Homer Circle has been associated with the fishing industry for almost 65 years. He started working in a sporting goods store after graduating from high school. Within a few years, a local newspaper asked him to take on the responsibility of being a sports editor. His personable style and great sense of humor created an immediate rapport with his audience.

A well-known but struggling lure-maker company, Heddon Lures, soon discovered Homer and encouraged him to join the company. James Heddon used Uncle Homer's creative mind and fishing knowledge to help propel his company into one of the top tackle manufacturers in the world. Unfortunately, there was a cost involved in this swift success—Uncle Homer's health.

We are all tempted by something. For some it is sensual pleasure. Others lust after material possessions. And for some, like Uncle Homer, the temptation is to try to be Superman.

Homer realized that the pace of his life needed to be modified and his stress reduced. It was no surprise when *Sports Afield* magazine asked Homer to come onboard and become their fishing editor that he accepted the invitation. Homer knew he would have a chance to work with talented fishermen from all over the country while perfecting his unique writing style. He also knew it was an opportunity to work on his sin of trying to be the messiah of the fishing world.

After 32 years, *Sports Afield* continues to be among the top outdoor magazines. This is due in part to the innumerable anglers who enjoy the relaxing way Uncle Homer tells a story.

One of my favorite fishing stories comes from a fable Homer put together. Here it is, in his own words:

> One April morning, the kind when there's a snap in the air and the smell of spring takes your breath away, I was walking around the shoreline of a lake, trying to make my mind up whether to go fishing or just stand there and love everything God created.
>
> Well, being the kind of guy I am, fishing won out, and I launched my boat. The creek I had a mind to fish was directly behind the cabins. So I didn't have to disturb the serenity God had created that morning.
>
> Deep into the creek, I moved along the channel, casting at everything in sight and just cranking that bait as hard as I could. Then something caught my eye. On the end of a log that jutted out in the creek was an acorn, so delicately balanced that it was a wonder that the slightest breeze hadn't blown it into the water.
>
> I stared at that acorn for what might have been a few minutes or maybe longer when a plump squirrel

came running down a tree. The critter spotted the acorn, eyed it for a moment, and then scampered out along the log. Tiptoeing to a halt, the squirrel snatched up the acorn with his front legs, got up on his hind legs, and proceeded to start eating.

Faster than I ever saw anything happen, the water under the end of that log exploded. A huge large-mouth bass rose up and, in one bite of its monster jaws, swallowed that squirrel whole.

I sat there in astonishment, feeling some sorrow for the poor little squirrel, but also realizing that it was all part of the law of nature. But then my thoughts were suddenly interrupted by the sight of that bass reappearing. This time the fish had an acorn in its mouth and placed it in the exact same position it had been before. Then he looked over at me, winked and smiled, and with a swirl of water, disappeared back under the log![1]

Uncle Homer's passion for fishing has been a great encouragement to many champion fishermen. More importantly, he has been a steadfast model of integrity and honesty. A successful outdoor writer like Homer is regularly pursued by countless marketing folks who ask him to promote products that may or may not have value. The temptation to encourage readers toward a certain product can often provide the author with special benefits, not the least of which is money.

Some of us refuse to accept such offers, realizing that credibility and integrity cannot be bought. I remember once losing a job as a field writer for a large magazine because I refused to write about a product that was nothing but "smoke and mirrors."

Homer has consistently modeled great character and a desire to stay clear of the temptation to compromise his style or honesty. Maybe the lessons he has learned from fishing have helped him to better understand the problems of falling into temptation.

All Tied Up

One of the most viewed treasures of our time was developed by Glen Lau. He utilized the fishing experiences of Uncle Homer and a few professional fishermen to develop the storyline. The movie *Big Mouth* has allowed anglers the opportunity to taste what life is like for a black bass. During the filming of this classic, Uncle Homer experienced some of the best fishing available in spring-fed Florida ponds and lakes.

While filming at Santee Cooper, Uncle Homer had finished his part and ventured off to do some fishing without the cameras rolling. Homer put on his chest-high waders and was working his way along the weedy shoreline. The water was only about an inch below the top of his waders as he slid his feet cautiously along the bottom.

He flipped his plastic Texas-rigged worm along a lily pad. The line jumped and Homer quickly reared back, only to pick up a bunch of slack. He paused momentarily to determine whether the fish spit the worm out or was racing toward him. As Homer continued to quickly reel in the slack, he recognized that the line was heading directly for his feet. With the ability of a rodeo calf roper, the spunky bass tied two half-hitches around Homer's feet.

The bass continued to tug away at his newly captured prey. Homer tried to break the line by pulling his feet apart. There was no way he was going to break 20-pound test line with some kind of John Travolta move underwater. With lightning speed Homer grabbed his sheath knife and took a big breath while reaching for the tangled line. The sharp blade pierced the taut line.

The ten-pound bass sprang up out of the water about six feet away, shaking its head with the large plastic worm, just as Homer raised his head above the water surface. Homer recalls, "As the cold water was beginning to fill my waders and my head lifted out of the water, I saw the fish jump right in front of me. It was as if he nodded at me and said, 'So long sucker.' "

It is a tremendous experience to listen to Uncle Homer's wonderful stories. Each time I am at a tackle manufacturers convention, I seek out Homer so I can listen and learn from him. His gentle spirit and soothing advice comes from a life filled with testing and trials.

One of the common threads connecting Homer's stories is his use of the plastic worm. Many anglers overlook the natural appearance of a well-constructed worm. A plastic worm can imitate natural foods such as salamanders, night-crawlers, lizards, eels, minnows, and leeches. Worms come in all sizes, shapes, and colors, but all have one thing in common—they really *tempt* the fish.

Few bass can withstand the temptation of a finely colored, slithering worm as it works its way over roots, trees, brush, and weeds. In the hands of a patient angler, a worm can creep along the bottom structure in a most alluring fashion.

Bombarded by Temptations

Temptation is something we all face in one form or another. We can be tempted in the flesh with illusions of sensual pleasures. Lust of the flesh can include both dietary and sexual fantasies. Another powerful force is a temptation of the mind. We can be tempted with thoughts of power, fame, and position. Finally, we can be tempted in the spirit. Our very soul can be attacked by Satan as he wages war on us.

Temptation comes when we are enticed, tested, or tried by our own lusts. The word *entice* is from a Greek hunting and fishing term meaning "to catch in a snare or trap," or "to lure a fish from his hiding place." The first-century disciples used a hook and line as well as nets to catch fish. They were only too familiar with the term and its seductive nuances. Being successful in their occupation depended upon using alluring methods to trap fish or make them bite.

In many ways the ardent angler is much like the ultimate tempter. He uses beguiling approaches to charm the fish into thinking his offerings are the real thing. By imparting certain movements to the rod and varying reeling speeds, the offerings can aggravate even the most wary species. Elusion and camouflage aid the fisherman in hiding the deadly razor-sharp hooks awaiting the unsuspecting quarry.

Before the Citizens Against Angling come after me, I need to make sure my dedicated readers realize that hunting and fishing are part of God's plan for man's survival and enjoyment. My purpose here is simply to make the point that just as a wary fish can be fooled into making a deadly mistake, so can *we* be fooled by the master deceiver—Satan. It is never God who tempts us: "When tempted, no one should say, 'God is tempting me.' For God cannot be tempted by evil, nor does he tempt anyone; but each one is tempted when, by his own evil desire, he is dragged away and enticed" (James 1:13-14).

Our minds are bombarded with daily temptations. The greater the temptation, often the more difficult it is to maintain a calm, relaxed pace. The inner stress becomes intense as we struggle through the inducements that tantalize our emotions.

Kay Arthur, in her wonderful book *His Imprint My Expression*, helps us better understand our dilemma:

> Life is hard, and the world's way out is often very appealing. We're tempted—tempted on every hand. People—even many who profess to know Christ—are weakening. And the aftermath is horrible and destructive—to the church, to our nation, to our homes, to our individual lives. And so, with every trial there is also

the potential of sin. The potential of yielding to the flesh connection. The potential of yielding to temptation.[2]

How can we cope with this onslaught of temptations? Many fishermen seek out those quiet, lonely waters to restore and refresh their spirits—to have some quality time with God. It is in these silent places that stress begins to flee from our bodies like a released fish. The stress of worrying about compromising our integrity to impress the boss and his clients melts away as the beauty of nature surrounds us. The fret over having just the right wardrobe to "look the part" for the business environment fades away. The temptation of dealing with the flirtatious attitudes of a coworker dissolve into the crisp, cool air surrounding a mountain lake. Our anxious desire to fixate on our bank account balance becomes unimportant as we focus on God's perspective and His majestic creation.

Being in God's great outdoors removes us from those unique trials and temptations. We can enjoy the freedom to listen to God without fax machines, doorbells, pagers, telephones, and voice-mail messages constantly distracting us from the quiet reflections and inspirations that only He can provide. During those special quiet times, free from the stress and tensions of the world, He can give us all we need to become spiritually rejuvenated.

But we must also live in the real world. For most of us the option doesn't exist for a permanent retreat to an environment that is free from external temptation. Temptation takes many forms—money, sex, power, perfectionism, machismo (the sense of being a tough guy), pride, materialism, greed, and slothfulness, just to name a few. Our lusts can dominate our lives if we allow them to. Much like that unsuspecting squirrel chasing after the acorn, we can suddenly find the jaws of sin around our throats, cutting off our spiritual breath. Lust has its power.

Men lust, but they know not what for;
They wander, and lose track of the goal;
They fight and compete, but they forget the prize;
They spread seed, but spurn the seasons of growth;
They chase power and glory, but miss the meaning of life.[3]

Money, Sex, Power

Richard Foster was right. In the mid-1980s he wrote *Money—Sex—Power*, a book that describes the human fascination with these three major temptations. They seem to ultimately embrace all other enticements. Perhaps if we could better understand these snares, protective spiritual barriers could then be erected to help fend off the stinging barbs of their unsuspecting hook.

The pull toward sin is something all humans experience—yes, even Jesus. "For we do not have a high priest who is unable to sympathize with our weaknesses, but we have one who has been tempted in every way, just as we are—yet was without sin" (Hebrews 4:15). As we study these areas of temptation, ask yourself the question, "How can I handle this area of my life with a Christlike perspective?"

The Love of Money

The desire to own, possess, and get rich is part of the American dream, right? But enough is never enough! I asked a millionaire friend of mine, "How much is enough?" He replied, "One million more than I had last week." We can easily get caught up in the rat race.

Some of us are like those fish who leave the quiet pool to journey out into the swift, moving stream. Suddenly they are swept along with all the other fish, frantically fighting for every morsel of food and molecule of oxygen just to stay alive.

For many people, money becomes the ultimate goal rather than a means to an end. Scripture warns us, "For the love of money is a root of all kinds of evil. Some people, eager for money, have wandered from the faith and pierced themselves with many griefs" (1 Timothy 6:10). Note carefully what the text says here. Money is not the root of all evil; rather, the *love* of money is.

Money can't buy health, happiness, respect, or the love of your family. Further, the more money you have, the more stress you have in trying to maintain your wealth. I find that more people can handle being poor than can properly handle being wealthy.

It requires a special committed disciple to properly handle wealth *and* the home. I know a few men who do an excellent job managing both. Someone once said, "Money can build a house, but it takes love to make it a home."

There is often something deeper in a person's heart than the pure motivation to make more money. For some, wealth becomes a way that they can prove self-worth. Some millionaires were abused as children and came from very humble beginnings. Having money may make them feel good about themselves.

For others money can provide a sense of power and control. Money can provide influence that might not otherwise be available. Rather than learning to skillfully manage people and problems, some find it easier to "leverage" respect with their financial status.

To some fishermen who have their priorities out of whack, money is something that has only one purpose—to assist with fishing activities. The definition of a pro bass fisherman with poor money-handling skills is "a guy who owns a $28,000 Ranger Bass Boat pulled by a $32,000 Chevy Suburban and has his family living in a $3,500 mobile home." The thing a little boy outgrows fastest is his allowance.

The basic question we must consider is, "Whose money is it?" The reality is, if you are a child of God, everything you have belongs to Him. In fact, Scripture teaches us that even the ability we have to make money comes from our heavenly Father (James 1:17).

Who, then, are we going to serve? The money gods or the God of all creation? Jesus said, "You cannot serve both God and money" (Luke 16:13). If we keep our focus on God and His plan for our lives, then we will obtain a proper perspective on the issue of money.

I know two men that God has blessed with substantial wealth. These men and their wives have given unselfishly to God's work and still have an abundance left over. God seems to continue to bless them more and more as they continue to give. They have possessions (some would call them expensive toys) that have been hard-earned and have been properly dedicated to God. They are used in His work and for His glory. These men will reach people who wouldn't normally be interested in talking with a person of lesser means.

If you struggle with the temptation of money, I suggest that you—

- Keep God's Word in your heart and read your Bible for guidance.

- Pray about your attitude toward money.

- Settle once and for all who you want to serve in your life—God or money?

- Develop some money-management skills.

- Make yourself accountable to a group of men as well as to your family.

The Seductive Lure of Sex

Sex can bring great blessing or incredible destruction. It all depends on whether it is done God's way. One insightful author explains:

Sex has enormous power. It is power to create and sustain community. Power to live in love. Power to know another deeply. Power to express the image of God. It is both a gift and a profound blessing from the Lord of love.

If perverted, sex is a power that destroys. It holds men captive. Turns quickly to an obsession. Burns with lust. It demeans human beings, reducing them to things to be used, abused, and discarded. Held in its bondage, otherwise reasonable men will lie to themselves and others, turn their hearts and minds away from God, leave their wives and the children they love, and choose to live in tension, guilt, and shame, all for the promise of tasting again the brief, pulsing current of its seductive pleasure.[4]

For some, sex is an issue of control, power, or manipulation. For others it can become an addiction that is fed with pornography, an affair, and fascination. The truth is that sensual pleasures brought about by lustful encounters outside of marriage also bring with them the pain of heartache and brokenness (Proverbs 2:18-19).

God ordained marriage and provided sex for procreation and enjoyment (Genesis 2:22-24; Song of Songs). God's counsel governing sexual relations is very clear. It is *never* to be engaged in outside the marriage relationship (1 Corinthians 7:1-5). Adultery is forbidden! Jesus was so concerned about the moral fabric of His followers that He instructed them to keep even their thoughts pure:

You have heard that it was said, "Do not commit adultery." But I tell you that anyone who looks at a woman lustfully has already committed adultery with her in his heart. If your right eye causes you to sin, gouge it out and throw it away. It is better for you to lose one part of your body than for your whole body to be thrown into hell (Matthew 5:27-29).

Once I gave my life to Christ, He began a process of inspiration and correction. God regularly gave me verses to guide my thinking and test my actions. In this area one verse stands out above all others: "No temptation has seized you except what is common to man. And God is faithful; He will not let you be tempted beyond what you can bear. But when you are tempted, He will also provide a way out so that you can stand up under it" (1 Corinthians 10:13).

What sexual temptation is facing you? God is faithful and able to sustain you if you are willing to be obedient to His calling. Temptation is common to all men and women. If we flee from the temptation (1 Corinthians 6:18) and ask God to control our passions and attitudes, He will help us refocus our thoughts. Remember, we can't focus on two things at once. If we focus our thoughts and actions on the things of God, then we leave no room for Satan's dirty footprints to walk through our hearts and minds (Luke 8:12).

If you find yourself being reeled-in by this temptation, I suggest you immediately contact your pastor, a trusted Christian friend, or a counselor. Ask them to help you deal with this problem. With their assistance, create a positive approach to problem-solving before you are hooked, filleted, and fried.

The Pursuit of Power

> If others are as powerful as we, what's the point of having power? It's only good as long as it puts us above and beyond our fellow human beings.[5]

Misdirected power is about ego, position, and status. It is evidenced in manipulation, deception, and destruction. Positive power can be used for good and creativity. But abuse of power can become a temptation that will defile our Christian witness quicker than you can possibly know.

The temptation for power is nothing new. Even Jesus had to deal with it among His disciples. James and John argued over who would be at the right side of Jesus when He went into glory (Mark 10:35-45). That attitude clearly betrayed a yearning for power and position.

As only Jesus could do, He called them to consider power and position from a perspective of "kingdom leadership." He said,

> You know that those who are regarded as rulers of the Gentiles lord it over them, and their high officials exercise authority over them. Not so with you. Instead, whoever wants to become great among you must be your servant and whoever wants to be first must be slave of all. For even the Son of Man did not come to be served, but to serve, and to give His life as a ransom for many (Mark 10:42-45).

Jesus taught that the kingdom style of leadership is servanthood—not a title, not position, and not fame. Jesus emptied Himself in humility and took on the role of a slave—a servant-leader. He never took advantage of another person's weakness. He always acted out of love and support. We are called to do the same.

Dealing with Temptations

Throughout Christ's ministry, He asked His disciples to constantly be on the alert for temptation. Many cautions were issued by our Master. Overcoming temptation must have been paramount in His mind, for why else would He have chosen to make reference to it in the lesson He taught His followers on prayer: "Lead us not into temptation, but deliver us from the evil one" (Matthew 6:13). And again, at the end of His earthly ministry, He cautioned: "Watch and pray so that you will not fall into temptation. The spirit is willing, but the body is weak" (Matthew 26:41).

I believe there is nothing more wary and vigilant than German brown trout in a small meandering stream. Their watchful eyes seem to detect any unnatural movement or disruption. Their alert body position and discrete feeding habits can confound the skill of even the most talented angler. The German brown trout is not easily fooled or tempted.

So it is with committed Christians. They will stand alert and watchful, carefully discriminating between those things that are real and pure, and those that are fake and artificial. The things that radiate eternal truth will attract the believer. Conversely, the artificial enticements of the world can be detected upon close inspection. The blemishes of sin can be seen through the microscope of patience, discretion, and guidance from the Holy Spirit.

Uncle Homer will tell you that trophy brown trout grow big because they have learned not to be enticed, lured, and suckered in by the temptations of their environment. Likewise, *we* can grow strong in our faith if we will learn to be patient with God and remain obedient to His Word.

Personal Growth

• Does money *drive* you or *free* you? Can you think of personal illustrations of each type of motivation in your life?

• How do the following verses speak to you about money issues?

> Matthew 6:24
>
> Luke 12:16-31
>
> 1 Timothy 6:10
>
> Luke 16:13
>
> 1 Peter 5:2

• What pressures in our society have caused you to stumble sexually? How can you avoid them in the future (for example, R-rated movies, television, magazines, flirtatious people)?

- How is power projected in your life? Can you think of positive and negative examples of how power is used?

- What is the "kingdom approach" to leadership in your situation?

PERSONAL PROFILE

Homer Circle

Background—Born and raised by a single-parent mother in Ohio. Fascinated with the outdoors from childhood. Presently one of the most respected anglers in the world. Worked with Glen Lau on several excellent fishing videos. One of the top outdoor columnists in the United States.

Age When First Fish Caught—12 years old.

Favorite Bible Verse—Matthew 7:12.

Family—Wife, Gayle, one daughter, four grandchildren, two great-grandchildren.

Favorite Fishing Hole—Any new lake.

Favorite Fishing Lure—Plastic worms.

Preferred Equipment—Bait casting with six-foot rod.

Most Respected Fishing Pro/Mentor or Instructor—Glen Lau.

Personal Comments—"Keeper memories are built through the heart."

10

Walking in Integrity

Fishing with Hank Parker

The sound of the car door closing woke Hank up to the reality that he had a hard three-day drive ahead of him to reach Lake Mead, Nevada. He would be alone with his thoughts and the parting words from his family regarding his priorities and his commitment to fulfilling his role at home.

It had been a tough two years. Success had taken its toll on his health and family. Shortly after winning his second Bass Masters Classic (1979) and Angler of the Year (1983), his popular television show began to skyrocket. The phone had also started ringing off the hook with more offers for public appearances than he could possibly accept.

Hank's pleasing personality, and his desire to accommodate everyone, led him to positively consider each request. The rigors of his schedule were now impacting the thing he cared for most—his relationship with God and family.

Hank arrived at Lake Mead to find the clear water and hot days that are typical for this reservoir. This kind of lake environment doesn't make for good fishing for someone (like Hank) who spends most of his time fishing shallow, murky impoundments.

Hank and I had enjoyed a good relationship for several years prior to this tournament in the spring of 1988. He had been on our Fellowship Of Christian Anglers Society (FOCAS) board of directors, and we had shared several meals during the sports shows we attended. As I saw Hank in the audience at the (FOCAS) evening Bible study where I was speaking, it became clear to me that something was bothering him. Knowing my background of fishing western clear-water impoundments, Hank asked me after the Bible study if I could recommend any particular bait or approach. His pre-fishing hadn't gone well and he was concerned about how he would do in this critical tournament.

I invited Hank back to my room and proceeded to dig out some of my "California Sissy Baits" that none of the "good ol' boys" would be caught dead with. Our western "finesse fishing methods with soft plastics" hadn't really caught on at that time in this area of the country.

After handing him a bag of gitzits, four-inch worms, and some lightweight sinkers, I asked him if things were going well with his career and family. His eyes filled up with tears as he proceeded to tell me and my wife, Louise, about the frustration he was going through.

Hank is known for his honesty and sincerity. His integrity and character are well-respected within the industry. Yet he was failing miserably with the people who really mattered—those in his all-important family circle.

He went on to describe his battle with hypocrisy. The idea of knowing what was the right thing to do while not doing it was beginning to eat away at his spirit like a cancer.

Hank went out the next day and competed, but our conversation lingered in his mind as he tried to make sense of it all. He sat back and let his partner develop most of the fishing strategy while he tried to figure out what to do about the hypocrisy in his life.

The results for the day were disappointing and reflected the work of an unfocused fisherman. The second day, however, brought new hope as God continued to help him resolve his personal conflicts. He awoke with a fresh sense of victory over his personal situation. Inasmuch as he liked tournament fishing, he decided this would be his last year of fishing the circuit. He had determined that he was going to be the dad he had always talked about being.

Hank took over the controls of his Ranger boat and directed it into some off-colored water he discovered during one of the practice days. He broke out his jigs and started working the brush. One by one, chunky bass filled his livewell. He weighed-in the heaviest stringer of the tournament and became a contender. By the end of the last day Hank had another nice limit of fish, enough to capture ninth place overall in the tournament.

His placing in the money, as well as having resolved his inner conflicts over character issues, allowed Hank to become more focused and develop a sense of urgency for his last year of competition fishing. The result was that he became the first "Bass Grand Slam" money winner of all time. Within a single year, he won the Super Tournament, Angler of the Year, and the BASS Classic. This was an accomplishment that propelled him to the top of the industry.

In the boat at the awards ceremony was his lovely wife, Angie. Hank had also won the battle for his family. They once again respected him as a man of honor, a man of integrity.

A Rebellious Kid

Hank will tell you he has lost more tournaments than he's won. He would also tell you the reason why character is presently so important to him. When he was young, he had anything but good character. He was a loser.

For starters, Hank's father was an alcoholic while his mother abused prescription drugs. As a result of the neglect and confusion he experienced, he became a "hell-raising" hot-tempered young man with a real taste for alcohol.

Hank was willing to settle for whatever felt good. His wild lifestyle was all that mattered to him. He was lost and angry. His future looked bleak.

Just about the time when life didn't seem worth living, his father became transformed in 1971 by accepting Jesus Christ as his personal Savior. Hank didn't think it would last. After all, his dad had been promising to quit drinking for years. Hypocrisy had been consistently modeled to him by his father.

His dad kept the faith, however, and continued to share with Hank that he was "saved" and born again. He was not only saved eternally, but also saved from living out the rest of his life in the drunken ways he'd known till now. He was saved from destroying his life, his family, and the lives of those around him. He was saved from continuing to be a hypocrite to all who knew him.

This modeling of Christ's power in his dad's life was strong, but not strong enough to motivate Hank to change. So he continued in his reckless ways.

In 1975 Hank's dad was killed in a tragic car accident. Relatives found a note that he had stuck inside the pages of his Bible requesting that when he died, he wanted "a memorial service where the gospel would be preached." He had written, "I have two sons who are lost and it might be the last time that they would ever hear what God says about being saved."

During the memorial service, Hank became so convicted about the sinful state of his life that he felt like he was going to explode. The preacher gave an altar call and Hank carefully considered the invitation. "I distinctly felt that God was trying to get through to me," he recalls. "It was as if He was saying, 'Hank, you've had your chances. I've knocked on your door before. Today you've been issued an ultimatum—you can believe that Jesus died as your substitute or you can keep going the way you're already headed and end up in hell.' "

Hank had run out of excuses. He knew the message: Jesus Christ had died for him. The living God had shed blood at Calvary that all humankind might repent and receive Him as Savior. He had taken our burdens and sin so that we might have eternal life. Hank could sense God saying to him, "Everything that you *want* to be and everything that you *can* be through Jesus is waiting for you. Or, you can go on living a hypocritical life and walk away. It's up to you."

Suddenly all the Scripture verses his dad had memorized and openly shared flooded into Hank's mind: "There is no one righteous, not even one; there is no one who understands, no one who seeks God" (Romans 3:10); "All have sinned and come short of the glory of God" (Romans 3:23); "For God so loved the world that He gave His only begotten Son that whosoever believes in Him should not perish, but have everlasting life" (John 3:16).

Hank went forward that day and his life has never been the same. He began a life of discipleship and put integrity at the top of his list of character traits to work on. His believable character and faith in God is what has helped make *Hank Parker Outdoor Magazine* one of the top fishing television programs in the country.

The Word Is Integrity

Hanging proudly in our hallway, between our sons' Eagle Scout plaques and their Merit Badge collection, is a letter from our friend Chuck Swindoll. Chuck could not attend their Eagle Court of Honor. Instead he provided an encouraging letter that has become a keepsake in our home. It is displayed for all to be reminded that the hallmark of a Christian's character is a life of integrity. Consider his words:

Your being awarded the highest rank in the Boy Scouts of America deserves special recognition. I commend you for this achievement, which represents discipline and determination in both of your lives. I join your parents and extended family in a warm embrace of affirmation.

Such an achievement underscores my confidence in today's youth. While prophets of doom swarm the media today, implying that the presence of wrong among so many adolescents means the absence of character in all, young men like you put those exaggerations in perspective. You and others like you, Dan and Tom, cause adults like me to look more hopefully on our nation's future. You give us renewed courage as we focus on the challenges of tomorrow.

And now, if I may . . . an important reminder. Years ago, Major General Dean was facing what he supposed was certain death from his communist captors during the second winter of his captivity in Korea. He was allowed only a few minutes to write his family a farewell message. In the eight or nine lines of his letter, he directed this one to his only son, "Tell Bill the word is *integrity*."

And so it remains, Dan and Tom. The word is not success; it is not fame, fortune, power, or pleasure. Never forget that, my young friends! Never allow anything to compromise your integrity.

As God directs your steps, uses your lives, expands your influence, and enables you to achieve even greater accomplishments, may you continue to conduct your lives in an exemplary manner. I am truly proud of you this day.

Remember, Dan and Tom, the word is *integrity*.

There are precious few individuals who consistently model the integrity they preach about. Perhaps the most consistent model of this trait I know is Chuck Swindoll, himself a fisherman. In what follows, I want to share some of the insights on integrity I've gleaned from this man's teachings over the years.

Did We Lose Our Way?

Disgrace and scandals fill the headlines of our daily newspapers. Reporters seem to revel in broadcasting the moral failures and indiscretions of world leaders. The church is not exempt. Well-known televangelists and some local pastors have removed themselves from ministry because of moral lapses.

One of the greatest hindrances to integrity today is hypocrisy. What cancer is to the human flesh, hypocrisy is to the church. It eats away at the vital parts of the body until it has finished its ugly work.

Hypocrisy was severely criticized by Jesus. The Sermon on the Mount is one example of how Jesus tried to warn His disciples about the dangers of straying from good character. Over and over again He warned His listeners to *not* be caught up in hypocrisy.

In its original form the word *hypocrite* referred to someone who hid behind a mask—one who put on a show. The word was also used of a person with an evil heart who hid behind a screen of godliness.

Today we become outraged when we discover that we are dealing with a hypocrite. People feel betrayed when the person they trusted has taken advantage of them. The opposite is also true. When we encounter someone who is authentic and genuine (a person with good character), we are drawn to them.

Chuck Swindoll, in a message delivered nearly a decade ago to his Evangelical Free congregation, suggested the following definition of character: "Character is the moral, ethical, and spiritual undergirding that rests on truth that reinforces a life, and that resists the temptation to compromise."[1] If a disciple lacks good character, all other spiritual traits and qualities will be ultimately seen as meaningless.

There is nothing more critical than to practically apply God's Word through righteous living. We need to *say what we mean* and *mean what we say*. An old country preacher put it this way: "Be who you is, cuz if you ain't who you is, you is who you ain't." What he was really saying is, Let's get real. Let's eliminate hypocrisy in our lives.

The Message from the Mount

People often compromise their integrity today because they operate from a mindset of "following the crowd"—that is, they listen more to others than they listen to God. They are more concerned with "being like them" than "being like Him" (God).

As the following Scripture passage demonstrates, many of the Jews' ancestors had previously listened *to others* instead of *to God*, even though God had warned them against this.

> Speak to the Israelites and say to them: "I am the LORD your God. You must not do as they do in Egypt, where you used to live, and *you must not do as they do* in the land of Canaan, where I am bringing you. *Do not follow their practices.* You must obey my laws and be careful to follow my decrees. I am the LORD your God" (Leviticus 18:2, emphasis added).

People of integrity have values they staunchly hold to, regardless of the cost. Are you willing to forsake the crowd and "not be like them"—even when your choice has a price? Count the cost—discipleship may not come cheap, but it's worth every sacrifice!

When Christ was delivering His Sermon on the Mount, one of His purposes was to communicate what is required to have a godly character (to be "like Him"). To be a faithful, committed disciple who has honor and good virtue, Jesus asked His followers to receive and act upon the "declarations of blessedness" (the Beatitudes):

Blessed are the poor in spirit, for theirs is the kingdom of heaven.

Blessed are those who mourn, for they will be comforted.

Blessed are the meek, for they will inherit the earth.

Blessed are those who hunger and thirst for righteousness, for they will be filled.

Blessed are the merciful, for they will be shown mercy.

Blessed are the pure in heart, for they will see God.

Blessed are the peacemakers, for they will be called sons of God.

Blessed are those who are persecuted because of righteousness, for theirs is the kingdom of heaven.

Blessed are you when people insult you, persecute you and falsely say all kinds of evil against you because of me. Rejoice and be glad, because great is your reward in heaven, for in the same way they persecuted the prophets who were before you (Matthew 5:2-11).

I love the progression Jesus provides in this fifth chapter of Matthew. Once our character reflects what He describes in the Beatitudes (verses 2-12), we are now prepared to be the "salt of the earth" and the "light of the world" He has called us to be (verses 13-14). Do we need to be perfect? I hope not, because I sure won't be eligible. We are to be *in process*— daily committing and rededicating our lives to the living God, asking for His forgiveness and divine guidance so we can grow and mature in our faith and integrity.

Holding Firm

Colossae had been a leading city in Asia Minor for several hundred years before Paul's day. But with the development of Laodicea and Hierapolis, Colossae's grandeur had diminished somewhat.

Through the ministry of Paul and Epaphras, a community of believers was established in Colossae. This young church soon became the target of heretical attacks and was in need of encouragement. Paul wrote to these believers,

> For this reason, since the day we heard about you, we have not stopped praying for you and asking God to fill you with the knowledge of His will through all spiritual wisdom and understanding. And we pray this in order that you may live a life worthy of the Lord and may please Him in every way: bearing fruit in every good work, growing in the knowledge of God (Colossians 1:9-10).

What was Paul saying here? He was telling the Colossian believers to hold firm to their character, to stay strong in their integrity. He was telling them that God would fill them with His spirit and power. Paul's encouragement to them was to *keep focused on God* and not worry about the attacks and persecutions that might come from those who were trying to destroy the church with dissenting views.

The question all *of us* need to ask is, Who are we serving? The believers in Colossae needed to be reminded that they should be abiding in God, not man or the self-serving gods of man. Paul said, "Am I now trying to win the approval of men, or of God? Or am I trying to please men? If I were still trying to please men, I would not be a servant of Christ" (Galatians 1:10). Christian integrity involves wholehearted commitment to God.

Building Character

Most of the nation's great fishermen can tell you hundreds of thrilling stories of the trophy fish they "tricked" with their skillful fishing presentations. These same fishermen can also tell you about the many near-death experiences which taught them lessons that eventually improved their skills and abilities. They could spend literally hours talking about all the fish they lost due to faulty equipment or poor judgments they made. The important thing is that they became better fishermen as a result of these experiences.

Adversity is something most of us tend to avoid. We seek those quiet places that are free from conflict and disruption. I have come to understand that pain is often necessary! We don't like it and it can present uncomfortable feelings, but it helps purify and refine our character.

Related to this, the apostle Paul provides this good counsel:

> Since we have been justified through faith, we have peace with God through our Lord Jesus Christ, through whom we have gained access by faith into this grace in which we now stand. And we rejoice in the hope of the glory of God. Not only so, but we also rejoice in our sufferings, because we know that suffering produces perseverance; perseverance, character; and character, hope (Romans 5:1-4).

I like how The Living Bible paraphrases Romans 5:4: "Patience develops strength of character in us and helps us trust God more each time we use it until finally our hope and faith are strong and steady." Is your character strong and steady?

Jesus perfected His character, from the perspective of His humanity, through His suffering. We read in Hebrews 5:7-9:

During the days of Jesus' life on earth, He offered up prayers and petitions with loud cries and tears to the one who could save Him from death, and He was heard because of His reverent submission. Although He was a son, He learned obedience from what He suffered and, once made perfect, He became the source of eternal salvation for all who obey Him.

In my own life I have seen the truth of how character is built through suffering, pain, and conflict. Pastor Swindoll often recounts one of the most important truths he learned in seminary: "God can't use you greatly until He has hurt you deeply!" What a great truth.

Be on Guard

A good fishing hole is not permanent. Over time the topography changes, water currents become redirected, vegetation decomposes, and fluctuation patterns have their cumulative effect on a good fishing spot. A fisherman must constantly evaluate his knowledge of the lake while practicing his skills to keep sharp and competitive.

We cannot blindly assume that character will always be with us without any effort on our part. Our recent history is filled with examples of people who had a moral lapse and now must live out their remaining days in the quiet shadows of embarrassment.

Scripture abounds with stories of the "heroes of the faith" who dealt with character issues. Hebrews 11 has chronicled some of these individuals and placed them on review for all to see. Names such as David, Abraham, Noah, Moses, Isaiah, Gideon, and Samuel are among the many mentioned. At different times in their lives, these great men of God had temporary lapses in integrity; however, they each recognized their failures, repented, and ended up with a refined character.

Don't let the politicians and media-manipulators fool you. *Character is everything!* They would like for us to believe that it is the policies or programs, or perhaps the "image" of a person, that is important. This is a complete lie! It is more important to be a God-fearing person than to be "politically correct." As the psalmist put it, "Let the Lord judge the peoples. Judge me, O Lord, according to my righteousness, according to my integrity, O Most High" (Psalm 7:8).

We also read in the Psalms:

> Blessed is the man who does not walk in the counsel of the wicked or stand in the way of sinners or sit in the seat of mockers. But his delight is in the law of the Lord, and on His law he meditates day and night. He is like a tree planted by streams of water, which yields its fruit in season and whose leaf does not wither. Whatever he does prospers. Not so the wicked! They are like chaff that the wind blows away (Psalm 1:1-4).

I don't believe it is any coincidence that the Psalms lead off with a verse on integrity! And this verse is an apt description of Hank Parker!

Hank is a great fisherman, father, and disciple. God has *broken* him greatly and now he can be *used* greatly. It was in the school of hard knocks that Hank discovered the virtue of character and the importance of keeping his word. He now pursues life from his heart rather than his pocketbook or mind. We would do well to imitate his example.

Personal Growth

- Who are your role models? Are they people of good character and integrity?

- What attributes of Christ do they most manifest?

- What kind of character do we need to be "salt and light" to a hurting world?

Personal Profile

Hank Parker

Background—Raised in North Carolina. Hosts the *Hank Parker Outdoor Magazine* television program. Winner of 16 national tournaments. BASS Classic winner 1979 and 1989; Grand Slam winner 1989.

Age When First Fish Caught—Five years old.

Favorite Bible Verses—1 John 5:12-13.

Family—Wife Angie, five children.

Favorite Fishing Hole—Sam Rayburn, Texas.

Favorite Fishing Lure—Mann's Bait-Hank Parker Model 3/4-oz. jig.

Preferred Equipment—Bait Casting.

Most Respected Fishing Pro or Instructor—Tommy Martin and Jimmy Houston.

Personal Comments—"I thank God I'm not what I used to be."

11

The Courageous Heart

Fishing with Brent Jones

Courage is the price you must pay in order to be alive at the deepest level.[1]

—*Tim Hansel*

M ost people define courage in terms of being fearless, having a daring spirit that enables one to meet intimidating challenges head-on, or having true grit. The word courage comes from the French word *coeur* which means "to have heart." Just as the heart lies at the body's core, enabling other parts of the body to function, so courage is central to the Christian, empowering him or her to manifest other qualities of Christlike character.

To play effectively as a tight end in professional football, and be selected numerous times to play in the Pro Bowl, one must have courage. To be named a member of John Madden and Howie Long's "Tough Guy" team, one must earn that position. These are among the highest honors given in the National Football League—and both were attained by Brent Jones of the San Francisco 49ers.

A Determined Spirit

Brent had prepared well during the 1996 preseason. Several nagging injuries were on the mend and his stamina and strength were outstanding. He regularly worked out with wide receivers Jerry Rice, Terrell Owens, and Nate Singleton to increase his speed and timing.

The 49ers started the season a little slow, as did Brent. Only four passes had been directed to him, and the offense looked lethargic. After the Carolina loss, the 49ers vowed to turn things around. As they prepared for the Atlanta game, however, disaster struck for Brent. The sports section of the Sunday paper reported:

> The 49er tight end jinx has struck again. . . . Brent Jones is scheduled for arthroscopic surgery this afternoon to remove an old screw that came loose in his shoulder. Jones partially dislocated his left shoulder in a contact scrimmage Thursday when teammates fell on him.[2]

Brent had had a long history of injuries. He suffered a shoulder separation in college. Sometime later he was in a very serious automobile accident which damaged his neck. In 1995 he was hit hard, causing his knee to collapse, and had to be carried off the field. Time and time again, coaches, reporters, and doctors counted him down and out—*finished*. Each time, though, God provided a miracle and Brent displayed the courage that allowed him to return with more passion and persistence than ever.

A Man of Courage

As of this writing Brent is back at his position, making remarkable catches and runs. As the 49ers march on to yet another playoff series, folks stand in awe at the determination and courage this man has demonstrated throughout his life.

I've gotten to know Brent during this past year as he became involved in our ministry. And the more I've gotten to know him, the more it has become clear that he gives full credit for his success and understanding of courage to his dad, his granddad, and the Lord.

It was in the midst of some outdoor adventures that Brent learned the heart and soul of the men he most admired. His Granddad was a tennis pro and an accomplished athlete. His reputation as a great competitor earned him the title, "The Champ." His father's encouragement and commitment to doing a first-class job also seeded Brent's fertile mind and spirit.

Brent recalls a particular family outing when his granddad and father took him and his brother, Craig, on a fishing-canoe trip at Hat Creek, near the Bernie Falls area in California. It was one of those beautiful early summer days when they pushed off from the shore, waving good-bye to the ladies in the camp. Brent and his brother were in the middle, while granddad directed the canoe from the front.

They paddled for some time, anticipating that they would soon stop and try their luck with those infamous Hat Creek trophy trout. Brent's 12-year-old mind was taking in all of granddad's instructions, when suddenly an unexpected flow of current flipped the canoe on its side. "We came out of that canoe like three greased pigs," Brent recalls. The icy-cold water temporarily paralyzed the three as they tried to hang on to their gear with one hand and the side of the boat with the other.

The fast current pushed the men toward shore where they stumbled onto dry land. "Granddad did not come out of the water until everyone was safely onshore and the gear had been secured," Brent recalls. "After he recovered all our equipment, granddad guided us to an area where we caught several really nice trout. He wouldn't let us go back to camp empty-handed, wet, and licking our bruises. We continued to conquer our fears and accomplish the goal of catching some fish for dinner."

Brent had seen this feisty spirit before as he watched his grandfather participate in sports and attack his daily work. His fearless nature and courageous heart provided Brent with a model that would help propel his life forward.

Courage in the Game of Life

The biggest battle for Brent, however, was off the field. While drivenness, courage, and guts are admirable qualities in an all-American football player, they can stand in the way of a vibrant spiritual life. Brent realized he could only be successful in life if he placed Jesus Christ at the center of his universe. "God needed to be in control—not Brent! When I sought to do things in my strength, I usually failed. Things would really get out of whack when I tried to rely on my own wisdom and efforts."

When Brent finally accepted Jesus as his personal Savior and Lord, that is when things really got under control in his life. "The book of Proverbs is very clear on the issue of control: 'Trust in the Lord with all your heart and lean not on your own understanding; in all your ways acknowledge him, and he will make your paths straight'" (Proverbs 3:5-6).

The Righteous Are Bold as Lions

Someone once said, "Courage is not the absence of fear, but the conquest of it."[3]

There are at least two types of courage. First, there is courage in the sense of an attitude or ability to deal with anything recognized as dangerous, difficult, or painful instead of running from it. Second, there is courage in the sense of having boldness to do what one thinks is right. *Both* definitions fit the profile of Brent Jones.

Sports commentators routinely talk about the special courage Brent has shown on the field. It is truly inspiring to witness how he continues to overcome adversity and stare difficult situations in the face, only to work through them with commitment and integrity.

Brent is not alone among courageous heroes of the faith. I think of biblical heroes such as Joshua, who faced the trials of leadership; Abraham, who left his homeland to seek out a country for his people and offered his son Isaac as a sacrifice; Gideon, who faced the confederate armies of the Midianites and Amalekites; Daniel, who persisted in prayer despite a conspiracy to cast him into the lion's den; Nehemiah, who refused to take "no" for an answer in rebuilding the temple; Thomas, who was willing to die for Jesus; Paul, who went to Jerusalem despite his impression that imprisonment awaited him there; and David, who challenged the giant Goliath for the right to rule the promised land. Courage is truly a mark of many of the biblical saints.

A Courageous Shepherd

David is particularly worthy of our focus. He was the youngest of eight sons in the town of Bethlehem. Before he became a talented musician, poet, prophet, diplomat, statesman, and warrior, he was a homely young man, slight in stature, who shepherded a flock on his father's farm.

Through his confidence in God, this courageous lad decided to take on the nine-foot, nine-inch Philistine known as Goliath (you can read about it in 1 Samuel 17). Goliath's armor weighed more than 125 pounds. The point of his spear alone was as heavy as a shot put.

When Goliath hurled his challenge toward the Israelites, Saul and his men cowered in fear. A defeatist attitude permeated the ranks as the young warrior stepped forward to shout his defiance against Goliath and the Philistines.

Convinced of David's courage and faith, Saul gave him his blessing and tried to outfit him with armor. Instead,

David took his shepherd's staff, his sling, and five smooth stones from a stream and headed into battle.

This reminds me of Brent. Coach George Seifert saw within this young man that same determination, faith, and courage. And like David, Brent called upon "the name of the Lord Almighty" (1 Samuel 17:45) to be with him in his battles on the line of scrimmage. Because of Brent's obvious physical limitations due to his previous injuries, it was obvious that the glory for Brent's effectiveness on the field had to go to the Lord. It was the Lord who sustained him!

Lessons from the Battlefield and the Gridiron

What lessons can we learn from David and Brent—these two courageous men separated by thousands of years? How can we imitate them and thereby better equip ourselves for service? There are three insights I want to share.

Claim the Land and Victory for Jesus

In the land of Israel, on the football fields of America, and in the home or workplace, there may be those who, like Goliath, will try to "claim the land" for ungodly causes. By attitude or action, they will "defy the ranks of righteousness." They may even defy God. Rejection, judgment, passive hostility, and unforgiveness are just some of the ways that modern-day Goliaths torment God's army of believers. Persecution comes in many different forms.

On January 4, 1997 Brent Jones and the ailing San Francisco 49ers trotted out of the warm locker room onto a frigid Lambeau Field and thousands of hostile hometown (Green Bay) fans. Brent had just left a hospital bed where intravenous fluids were injected into his flu-sick body. As he entered the field, he asked the question in much the same way David asked of the Philistines: "Who are these foreigners?" And with the same courage, Brent went onto the field and played one of the most gallant games of his professional career. Unfortunately, *so did the Green Bay Packers*. The recipe of a hostile hometown crowd mixed with multiple mistakes and penalties by the 49ers allowed the stronger Packers to overwhelm the beat-up 49ers.

In the case of David, of course, it was different. Despite overwhelming odds, the much smaller David took one of his river stones and hurled it into the skull of the giant Goliath, killing him on the spot. When David asked, "Who is this uncircumcised Philistine?" he was alluding to the fact that this unregenerate ape of a man was not one of God's covenant people. The giant could expect no help from the Lord and thus should be defeated easily.

We learn a good lesson here. God can do more with one little committed person, willing to try, than with a whole army of hesitant soldiers.

Put on the Armor

King Saul tried to dress David in his armor. The weight and bulkiness of the leather and metal, however, were too much for David to handle. David's armor would be that of God's protection.

God provides armor for us as well:

Finally, be strong in the Lord and in His mighty power. Put on the full armor of God so that you can take your stand against the devil's schemes. For our struggle is not against flesh and blood, but against the rulers, against the authorities, against the powers of this dark world and against the spiritual forces of evil in the heavenly realms. Therefore put on the full armor of God, so that when the day of evil comes, you may be able to stand your ground, and after you have done everything, to stand. Stand firm then, with the belt of truth buckled around your waist, with the breastplate of righteousness in place, and with your feet fitted with the readiness that comes from the gospel of peace. In addition to all this, take up the shield of faith, with which you can extinguish all the flaming arrows of the evil one.

Take the helmet of salvation and the sword of the Spirit, which is the word of God. And pray in the Spirit on all occasions with all kinds of prayers and requests. With this in mind, be alert and always keep on praying for all the saints (Ephesians 6:10-18).

Trust in God, for the Battle Is His

David told Goliath, "I come against you in the name of the Lord" (1 Samuel 17:45). David knew who was on his side and how the battle would be won. God had given him a plan and a vision. God provided the strength and creativity for David to use the familiar to do the incredible.

Henry Ward Beecher once said of this incident, "Difficulties are God's errands. When we are sent upon them we should esteem it a proof of God's confidence and as a compliment from Him."[4]

What Is Your "Goliath"?

We all have times when we face a personal Goliath. There are situations in which the odds seem overwhelming against us. The possibility of winning the struggle seems futile. When that happens, we, like David, have nowhere to turn but to God. We too can meet that personal giant in the name of the Lord Almighty, the Creator of the universe, the Lover of our souls.

It was in God's name that David killed Goliath. It is with God's help that Christians through the ages have faced similar impossible situations and have emerged victorious.

What is the problem you face today, dear brother? Like David, are you calling upon God's mighty power and strength? Like Brent Jones, do you declare, "The Lord is the strength of my life; of whom shall I be afraid?" (Psalm 27:1 KJV).

You say, "But Jim, I *am* afraid!" Eddie Rickenbacker, who regularly pushed the envelope of discovery and exploration, once said: "Courage is doing what you're afraid to do. There can be no courage unless you're scared."[5]

Every time you approach a new challenge, look to God for His strength and power. Seek His counsel and move forward with courage. You will approach fear head-on, stare it down, and do the very thing you think you cannot. If it is of God, He will provide a way when there seems to be none.

Whether you are a professional football player or a couch-bound fan, your calling is a courageous one—to be a disciple of the living Lord and to help spread the Good News of His love in a hostile world.

Get in the game—play with courage.

Personal Growth

- What is courage? How does it manifest itself in your life?

- What are you fearful of? How can you gain victory over your fears? What insights do the following verses provide you on this subject?

> Proverbs 28:1
>
> Ezekiel 2:6
>
> Ezekiel 3:9
>
> 1 Corinthians 16:13
>
> Philippians 1:27-28
>
> 2 Timothy 1:7

- How did Daniel show courage (Daniel 4:27, 5:17-23, 6:10-23)?

- What does the apostle Paul teach about courage in 1 Corinthians 16:13?

PERSONAL PROFILE

Brent Jones

Background—Grew up in San Jose, California. Attended the University of Santa Clara, where his football career blossomed. After an all-American collegian career, he was drafted in the fifth round by the Pittsburgh Steelers. In 1987 he joined the San Francisco 49ers and proceeded to play in *and win* three Super Bowls and four Pro Bowls.

Age When First Fish Caught—Five or six years old.

Favorite Bible Verses—Proverbs 3:5-6.

Family—Wife, Dana, two daughters.

Favorite Fishing Hole—Hat Creek, California.

Favorite Fishing Lure—Black and Gold Panther Martin Spinners.

Preferred Equipment—Ultra Light.

Most Respected Fishing Pro/Mentor or Instructor—Jim Grassi.

Personal Comments—"Trust in the Lord always. He really knows what is best."

12

Perilous Pride

Fishing with Ron Shearer

People with pride often embellish fairly routine events to make themselves out to be something they are not. Such is the case with a guy who turns catching a four-inch minnow into a life-and-death battle with a cold-blooded monster fish that could have snapped his boat in half at any time but succumbed to the power and skill of the angler.

Ann Landers, the great theologian, once featured a poem in one of her columns entitled, "And God Said, No." It opens with a bit of wisdom on pride.

I asked God to take away my pride,
And God said, "No."
He said it was not for Him to take away,
But for me to give up.

This is not an easy thing to do, especially for fishermen. Men tend to be hunters by nature. They tend to be proud. If they are not hunting game, they will hunt success, accomplishment, or power. But Solomon warns, "Pride goes before destruction, and a haughty spirit before stumbling" (Proverbs 16:18).

Ron Shearer is a man who is well-acquainted with the struggle to give up sinful pride. We can learn much from him.

Seeking Success

Ron grew up with a father who stressed the importance of hard work. As a young boy he periodically needed a break from the many chores that were his responsibility on the family farm. He sought to hunt and fish as often as he could. It became his solace, his time to restore and refresh himself, and a time for his tender ego to heal from the hurtful words of driven parents.

His mother's favorite saying had been, "You will never amount to anything because all you want to do is hunt and fish." The resentment Ron built up for that statement over the years was the motivation that encouraged him to become one of the nation's most versatile outdoorsmen. It made him determined to make a living in the great outdoors.

With the fledgling bass circuit firing up, Ron saw a great opportunity to take his God-given fishing talents and put them up against some of his "country cousins." In 1978 he won his first national tournament. Pride exemplified Ron's character. Some called him arrogant. "I had a big head. Boy, I thought I was good."

Ron recognized that his exaggerated self-esteem and haughty spirit was not becoming of a man of God. Little by little, God impressed upon him the need to address this character flaw that had become sin in his life.

One such time was when he had the honor of doing a seminar with a legend in the fishing industry, Jimmy Rogers. Ron thought it might be a real opportunity for him to strut his stuff. Instead, that big ol' boy with the mild manner taught Ron a lesson he would never forget.

"I had just finished my part of the seminar," Ron recalls, "when Jimmy got up and started trick-casting. He was doing pretty good when a little girl arose from her seat and stepped into the aisle just when he released. To avoid hitting her he pulled his cast and backlashed his reel. Everyone looked around as if to say, 'I thought pros didn't do that.' I thought, 'Now I know my part of the seminar was better than his. Boy I'm good!' "

The seminar ended and Ron met a few of his friends. As they gathered to chat around a coke machine, Ron saw a fellow come up to Jimmy seeking some instruction on how to cast a bait-casting reel. Jimmy proceeded to take the fellow to the parking lot where it was about 15 degrees with spitting snow falling. Ron peered out the window and watched Jimmy talk to the young man, then saw this fellow promptly cast the rod *and* reel across the parking lot. Not just once but several times. Each time ol' Jim would calmly walk across the lot and pick it up.

After about ten minutes they came in. As Jimmy walked by, Ron said, "I've never seen a guy as bad at casting as that guy. He's never going to get it! Don't you think you're wasting your time with him?"

Jimmy smiled and calmly stated, "Well, maybe he won't ever be a great fisherman, but the only other thing I had to do was to stand in here, listening to all your fishing tales, and I've already heard all those lies. Let me ask you something. What did that cost me? Just time. Who knows how much time we have? Besides, when that guy walks into a tackle store and sees your picture and my picture on a product, whose do you think he will buy?"

Ron's friends looked at him as if he were a complete jerk—and he was. His pride and conceit had gotten the best of him. He realized that the kind of character and integrity Jimmy Rogers modeled is what Christianity is all about. Just as Jesus stopped what He was doing and took time for people, this great fisherman humbly used his gifts and talents to reach people.

Pride Before a Fall

Ron continued to fish bass tournaments and focused more and more on his character. Each time he thought he had overcome his sinful pride, some incident would set him up for a fall. One such incident occurred during a record-breaking tournament.

Ron was fishing a bass national tournament when he caught a legendary stringer of seven fish weighing 36.8 pounds at Lake Okeechobee, Florida. He caught the fish in 20 minutes, all on a Pet Spoon with a short white skirt over floating grass-beds.

That night Ron could hardly contain himself. "Having just weighed in the largest stringer of fish ever caught in a national tournament was cause enough to shower the audience with a prideful attitude. I was a real jerk."

The last day of the tournament Ron drew the very last starting place. After everyone had left, he raced to his favorite spot to find that the word had leaked out and 42 boats were sitting on the one-and-a-half-acre-grass-bed. "The throng of people were flinging lures all over that weed patch. These fish had grown big because they had sharper instincts than fish elsewhere on the lake. The fish realized the pressure on them and totally got lockjaw." *They weren't biting!*

At about ten o'clock, Ron realized that his prideful attitude might have cost him the tournament and that he had better do something quick. "I told my partner we needed to use a little all-in-good-fun trickery to get rid of those fishermen. We worked our way back to the mouth of the cove about 200 yards from where the fishermen were. I stood on my plastic worm that was on the deck of my boat. I struck back and started yelling for the dip net. My partner played it out perfectly as he charged to my end of the boat, reaching down into the water to dip out my imaginary fish. I leaned over the side as we pretended to scoop my fish out of the net. Because my body and the open door of the livewell were between the other fishermen and the imaginary fish, all they could see was excitement and not the fish."

Ron and his partner kept this act up for a half hour and sat back to watch virtually every remaining fisherman come out of the cove and crowd around his boat. The two "actors" (again, all in good fun!) took off and drove around the lake for about a half hour. With everyone's attention occupied on the new spot, Ron could sneak back into the old hole.

Now that the fish had settled down, it only took a few casts to intrigue the hungry fish. Ron boated enough fish to win the tournament. After it was all over, he reflected on the lessons he learned on the pitfalls associated with a prideful life. The words of the psalmist rang in his ears, "You save the humble but bring low those whose eyes are haughty" (Psalm 18:27).

Jonah—The Bait for a Big Fish

Tucked away in the latter part of the Old Testament is a little four-chapter book about a prophet named Jonah. The book of Jonah is an autobiography written after Jonah's visit to Nineveh. According to 2 Kings 14:23-25, Jonah was the son of Amittai and lived during the reign of Jeroboam.

As a prophet, Jonah became prideful of his spiritual gift and power. He had heard of the wickedness and barbarism of Nineveh, the capital of Assyria. He had prophesied the demise of the city and felt that his expertise could better be used elsewhere. Here's the dilemma he faced:

> If he went declaring a message of judgment and the people repented, God would show mercy, and Jonah's prophecy would be null and void. His credentials as a prophet in Jeroboam's court would be greatly devalued if not bankrupt altogether. Jonah clearly states in chapter 4, verse 2 that he fled to Tarshish because he knew God would show the Ninevites mercy if they repented.[1]

But then something unexpected happened—Jonah got swallowed by a fish. Whatever type of fish swallowed the prophet is open for debate. We know for certain only that it was a large fish, a great fish, perhaps a sea bass, giant grouper, or maybe even a whale (not a member of the fish family). This fish was on a mission for God—a mission to help the prophet learn humility and become the obedient prophet God had intended.

Once Jonah returned to Nineveh and proclaimed the message that God gave him, there was a massive revival there. This was the largest evangelistic crusade in history. Despite Jonah's apparent disapproval of God's plan to save this community, people were stirred to repentance—and all because pride was dealt with in a servant of God.

A Checklist for Prideful Servants

Dwight L. Moody once said, "God sends no one away empty, except those who are full of themselves."[2] Today it seems that many in our nation are "full of themselves." In his last letter to young Timothy, the apostle Paul reminded his disciple of the signs of the end times. I believe we are now living in those days, and see this prophecy by Paul as a registry of sins that can befall us when pride takes over.

> But realize this, that in the last days difficult times will come. For men will be lovers of self, lovers of money, boastful, arrogant, revilers, disobedient to parents, ungrateful, unholy, unloving, irreconcilable, malicious gossips, without self-control, brutal, haters of good, treacherous, reckless, conceited, lovers of pleasure rather than lovers of God; holding to a form of godliness, although they have denied its power; avoid such men as these (2 Timothy 3:1-5 NASB).

Sound familiar? Men who are lovers of self, boastful, arrogant—you know, guys who are full of themselves. If this type of person is unfamiliar to you, just visit the nearest lake the next time there is a fishing tournament. Stand close to the weigh-in table and listen to the braggers talk about what they did.

My experience as a successful tournament fisherman is that God should get most of the credit. After all, He gave us the ability and wisdom to figure those fish out. He directs the fish to respond to our offerings. He provides the very water that the fish live in. So what is there for us to boast about?

Both Ron Shearer and I have figuratively experienced living in the belly of a stinky fish on more than one occasion. Pride has been an issue that we've both struggled with.

A lot of what I've learned about pride has come from the Old Testament. Perhaps the following warnings will help motivate you just as they've motivated me:

- Pride is a hindrance to seeking God (Psalm 10:4; Hosea 7:10; Proverbs 26:12).

- Pride leads men to reject God (Jeremiah 43:2).

- Pride persecutes the Spirit of God (Psalm 10:2).

- Pride produces a contentious heart (Proverbs 13:10; 28:25).

- Pride involves self-deception (Jeremiah 49:16; Obadiah 1:3).

Ron and I are learning that the ultimate high is when *God* exalts His children. Self-adulation just leads to disappointment and humiliation. I believe Jesus said it best: "Whoever exalts himself shall be humbled; and whoever humbles himself shall be exalted" (Matthew 23:12 NASB).

Oh God, give us humble hearts.

Personal Growth

• What does this biblical statement mean to you: "Pride goes before destruction, and a haughty spirit before stumbling" (Proverbs 16:18)?

• The greatest miracle in the book of Jonah was the change in Jonah's prideful heart and his subsequent willingness to be used by God in Nineveh. How does your life compare to Jonah's?

• What does the Great Commission mean to you? Read Matthew 28:18. Are you being obedient to the call?

PERSONAL PROFILE

Ron Shearer

Background—Born and raised in Winchester, Kentucky. Grew up on a farm next to the Kentucky River. A former professional fisherman and one of the most versatile outdoorsmen in the country. His syndicated television show, *The Great American Outdoors*, is one of the most watched weekend programs. His passion for the great outdoors and his family remains strong to this day.

Age When First Fish Caught—Four years old (a four-pound bass).

Favorite Bible Verses—Matthew 7:15-20 and 1 Corinthians 15:10.

Family—Married to Michelle (a business manager). One son.

Favorite Fishing Hole—Kentucky Lake.

Favorite Fishing Lure—The lure I last caught a fish on—"be versatile."

Preferred Equipment—Bait Casting.

Most Respected Fishing Pro/Mentor or Instructor—Buck Perry.

Personal Comments—"God doesn't love us on a performance basis. People need to experience the inner peace of God."

The *Healthy* Christian Family

Fishing with Paul Overstreet

It was one of those beautiful Tennessee summer afternoons. The birds were chirping and the fish were jumping down by the meandering river located on the back side of the property. Paul Overstreet looked out his studio window and realized it was time to take a break from the consuming task of songwriting and recording. His five children—ages three, six, seven, nine, and ten—were frolicking on the lawn, anticipating some playtime with dad.

His thoughts went back to his own youth when times were not so joyous. He grew up in a poor area of Mississippi in a home that brought confusion to his impressionable mind. His dad was a Southern Baptist preacher, but was unable to strike a harmonic relationship with his mother. Early in their marriage, there was evidence that the union was doomed. Unfortunately, the notion of a supportive, unified family was soon to become a memory of brokenness and strife.

While Paul accepted the Lord at ten years of age, he had no positive role models or support to help him continue his walk with Jesus. He eventually fell captive to habits and behaviors that distracted him from a meaningful Christ-centered life.

His mother moved to John's Bayou Fishing Camp, and Paul starting spending a great deal of time alone in the swamps, fishing and hunting. While there, he often reflected on the importance of God, family, and the despair of his own situation.

Having caught his first fish at five years of age, Paul soon became a prodigy of his fishing grandparents and uncles who had a passion for the great outdoors. He quickly learned the skills required to achieve and survive.

Inspired Songwriter

Paul and his wife Julie had built a home on the peaceful Harpeth River outside of Nashville, Tennessee. It was important for the family to be away from the stresses and influences of the country music capital of the world. By having his studio and home at the ranch, he could now give his family the quality time and attention he did not receive as a boy.

Paul opened the door of his office and yelled for the kids to grab their poles. (He can call his rods "poles" because he lives in the Southeast.) He always enjoys the challenge of teaching his kids the fine art of fishing. "Kids are naturally squirmy—they don't like to sit still very long. With five of them, it's a full time job just keeping hooks baited and lines untangled," says Paul.

Paul preaches the same lecture each time they fish—instructing the kids to *settle down, keep still,* and *be patient.* On this occasion, his little six-year-old girl, Harmony, listened and obeyed. She focused on his instructions and was blessed by catching three nice fish. The small-mouth bass and two drum (bony fish) were released back into the water after an appropriate family celebration.

The other kids couldn't understand why Harmony had all the success. Paul continued to remind them that she was doing what he had said. The older kids were better casters, had more knowledge, and were more naturally gifted, but Harmony's obedience and patience paid off.

As the sun settled along the western tree-lined ridge, the smell of fried chicken began to fill the air. Paul helped the kids pack up and guided them in the direction of home. As he carried his youngest and grabbed hold of Harmony's hand, his heart was warmed with the reality of the moment. God had given him the thing in life he desired most—a family. Maybe Thomas Jefferson was right: "The happiest moments of a man's life are the few which you pass at home in the bosom of your family."

To the music industry and general public, Paul Overstreet is best known for his inspirational songwriting. His songs have advanced the careers of well-respected artists such as Randy Travis ("Forever and Ever Amen," "On the Other Hand"), The Judds ("Love Can Build a Bridge"), and Anne Murray ("I Fell in Love Again Last Night"), just to name a few. His own award-winning albums ("Heroes," "Sowin' in Love," and "Love Is Strong") have called the nation to reconsider the importance of traditional family values.

When Paul *truly* accepted Jesus as Lord and Savior in 1985, God began to encourage him with creativity and enthusiasm that led to Spirit-inspired music. His motivation came from his study of God's Word (especially Proverbs) and the realization that much of his early life had been frittered away—*wasted*. Paul recalls, "I allowed sin to destroy much of my youth—those days are gone, wasted. But God's promise found in Joel 2:25 tells me that He will restore the years 'the locusts have taken away.'"

"My family is the most important thing," Paul says. "I feel we have to fight to keep our families together. It's a war out there and Satan will win if we don't maintain traditional family values. Broken homes have become an acceptable standard, rather than the standard of God's plan for the family."

Paul wants his songs to bring a positive family message to people. He reflects:

> As a nation we seem to exalt whatever we can— often things that don't really matter. Music seems to glorify those values and causes we support. Folks get motivated by whatever is "hot."
>
> I hoped that if God allowed my songs to become a hit, then people could hear about the positive aspects of family and the importance of good role models. My song, "Heroes," lifted up *dad* as a true champion. When "Love Helps Those Who Cannot Help Themselves" became a hit, many folks realized the importance of faith and positive relationships.
>
> Most of my contemporaries have made a good living out of writing and singing "sad songs" or stories that talk about broken relationships. I want my music to help restore families and point to the positive side of life. We really need to make a conscious effort to make things better.
>
> One of the most important attributes of a disciple is how he treats his family. According to Timothy and Titus, the requirements for spiritual leadership start with the administration and care of our homes. When we consider spiritual traits, there is probably none more important than being a spiritual leader of the home.

Tell Me About the Good Ol' Days

It has been my privilege to travel the country and routinely provide positive messages on traditional family values. On several occasions my twin sons—both of whom are songwriters, performers, and pastors—open the service with some of the songs from their "Times to Cherish" album. While they have some original music on the album, one of the most requested songs is "Grandpa Tell Me About the Good Ol' Days," a song about families praying together, staying together, and loving each other.

Watching the audience join in on the chorus reaffirms my faith in God—that His plan for the family is still respected and promoted by most folks. Those great lyrics still ring in my ears.

Those "good ol' days" are still a sought-after model in our culture. According to two separate studies conducted in 1990, 97 percent of Americans indicated that having a good family was important to them. The irony of this statistic is that divorce rates have more than tripled since 1960. Nearly 60 percent of our youth will live in a broken home before they reach 18; one-third of our youth are latchkey children with no one to greet them when they come home from school; and births out of wedlock have increased by more than 450 percent since 1966.[1]

As a nation, our actions don't match our words. In a country supposedly bent on the pursuit of excellence, it is ironic that we often settle for "fair to even poor" when it comes to the family. If half our corporations or schools were collapsing, we would be in a panic. Truly, the basic institution of our culture—the family—is in a very fragile state today.

The way I see it, each nation is like a pier reaching out into the sea of civilization. Some anchorages are strong and secure; others are decomposing and frail. The basic foundation that holds those piers in place are the individual pilings, representing each family structure. As more and more homes disintegrate and crumble, the nation is in jeopardy of collapse. Historian Edward Gibbon was certainly right when he declared that one of the chief reasons for the collapse of Rome to the barbarians was the previous collapse of the Roman household!

In 1955 some 60 percent of American households with children living at home matched the "traditional family" model of a working father, a homemaking mother, and two or more school-age children. In 1980 this family model represented only 11 percent of American homes, and in 1985 it dropped to only seven percent.

Today we have a very high mobility due to so many job transfers. Many in our culture lack deep roots due to an absence of the extended family. While some women must work to provide the necessary resources to support a family, there are many more who work to acquire the extras in life at the risk of not having enough time with the family.

Many reading this chapter might believe I'm attacking individuals who are a product of a broken home environment. I'm keenly aware that many people have gotten married without knowing that the institution of marriage is a covenant between two individuals and God. I'm also aware that there are those who, for reasons that are beyond their control, cannot keep their marriages together. Some in our culture have felt the pain of a dysfunctional environment. And certainly, God did not intend for anyone to live in an abusive situation.

While the traditional family environment is what God ordained and established as an ideal, He provides grace for all who are truly repentant. Remember, even the first family was dysfunctional. Adam and Eve had their problems with rebellious kids and broken fellowship with God.

I believe that God's Word lays out the ideal family pattern—one that was used as a pattern for the formation of our great country. Obedience to God's Word allows a family to prosper and a nation to become great.

Paul Overstreet's experience that day on the bank with his little girl Harmony was indicative of what is needed between our heavenly Father and His children. We need to *listen and obey*. God wants to instruct us so we can receive the blessings He has ordained. He needs disciples willing to bend their knees and open their hearts. Then our nets will be filled with His wonderful benefits.

God's Plan for Healthy Families

A study of God's Word indicates that there are at least five characteristics common to healthy families: appreciation and encouragement, communication, time spent together, commitment, and spiritual development. Whether you have a traditional family, a single-parent family, or a blended family, God's Word points us to these traits and values that we might strengthen our homes and nation. Let's take a look at them in a little more detail.

Appreciation and Encouragement

Much of what we witness in the media is discouraging. We are bombarded with the claim that if we don't buy the right products, we won't smell good, our teeth won't shine, and our hair will fall out. The list is endless. Television programming is full of smart-mouth kids and uncaring parents who show little or no support or motivation for one another. It seems that the only time set aside to speak to one another in these shows is to trade insults.

When I look for an example of the ultimate encourager, I think of Jesus. Shortly after being filled with the Spirit at the Jordan River and spending some 40 days being tempted by the Devil in the desert, He walked along the shoreline of the Sea of Galilee encouraging His fishermen-disciples to join Him. He then returned to His hometown to announce the purpose of His calling.

In His messianic inauguration speech (taken from Isaiah 61), words like "proclaim," "free," "bind-up," "renew," "restore," "release," "enlighten," and "rebuild" can be found. Jesus came to save us, yes, but He also came to *encourage*, *revitalize*, and *uplift*. He is our supporter and comforter. His spirit will be our stronghold to empower us.

In their award-winning book *The Blessing*, Gary Smalley and John Trent discuss a number of ways we can encourage others. They suggest that balcony people, rooters, and enthusiasts can help reassure people of their importance and self-worth. They help inspire people to fully utilize their God-given gifts and talents.

Our values should come from an understanding that we are children of the King. We must remember that what we communicate to others can potentially encourage *or* discourage them. If moms and dads would provide as much positive interaction with their children as they render discipline, our kids could better accept the loving grace of a merciful God. Remember, a child's first impression of the character of God comes from the relationship they have with their own father.

If dad is a loving, kind, tender individual, they will see God as compassionate and loving. Unfortunately, some fathers have emotionally and physically abandoned their children, and this creates in them a sense of mistrust and anger toward God.

We can encourage our children in a variety of ways. For example, we can show an active interest in their priorities. Attend their events and programs as a visible sign of support. Ask probing questions about their feelings while being an attentive listener. Don't take on the role of the "Shell Answer Man," but instead help them to figure out answers to life's problems using God's Word and prayer as a means to discover God's perfect plan.

Another way to encourage our children is to picture a bright future. Encourage them by focusing on their potential. Help point to a positive direction that allows them to envision honorable goals that will help stretch their faith and encourage their trust in God. Assist them in identifying their spiritual gift(s) and provide the necessary time and resources to contribute in the nurturing of these gifts.

Most important, we need to show regular physical affection for our children. Psychologists tell us that kids need at least ten big hugs daily to displace the negativity inflicted by our often-cruel society. Let your kids know they are important by blessing them with a hug or kiss. My twin sons are 26 years old, and I still give them a hug and kiss on the cheek when we greet each other. Most "macho guys" feel it's unmanly to express genuine affection. *But they're wrong!* A real man is so sure of his sexual identity that he has no problem sharing his affection in tangible ways to both his daughters *and* sons.

One of the lessons I learned from my good friend Jimmy Houston is to share affection with everyone and everything. Jimmy kisses a lot of fish as part of his personality. I have made it a practice to have all first-time guests in my Ranger Bass boat kiss the first fish they catch. It provides for some interesting reaction and lively humor. It's also a great way to determine the gender of the fish before releasing it. If the fish is a female, she will pucker up before you kiss her. If he's a male fish, he'll pucker up after you kiss him.

Jesus felt that sharing affection was so important that He chastised His own disciples for their lack of sensitivity to children. People were bringing little children to Him, but the disciples rebuked them. When Jesus saw this, He was indignant. He said to them, "'Let the little children come to me, and do not hinder them, for the kingdom of God belongs to such as these. I tell you the truth, anyone who will not receive the kingdom of God like a little child will never enter it.' And he took the children in his arms, *put his hands on them and blessed them*" (Mark 10:13-16, emphasis added).

It is extremely important that we show our appreciation and encouragement by making sure others sense our unconditional love and support. There will be times when we are justifiably disappointed with our kids. We will be outraged and insulted over their actions and attitudes. But we must criticize *the action* and not *the actor*. Be quick to forgive, and provide guidance that demonstrates your concern and care. Don't dwell on past failures but project a positive corrective attitude toward the future.

There is no doubt that the apostle Paul caught Christ's vision. In a most difficult time in his life, he was still able to exhort fellow believers: "Therefore encourage one another, and build up one another, just as you also are doing" (1 Thessalonians 5:11).

Good Communication

An important way we can show appreciation and encouragement to others is through good communication. I enjoy traveling the South and Southeast because you can still see the old homes with a swing on the front porch. Life is paced a bit slower and people still use those front porches much the way they did 50 years ago. People often sit and chat on those porches.

When ours was primarily an agrarian culture, family members spent an average of five hours per day communicating with their young folks. According to many family experts, we now spend an average of 14.5 minutes per day with our kids, including 12 minutes for negative comments or assigning chores. Some studies show that American dads spend as little as 37.5 seconds per day in positive interactive communication with their kids. The communication between mothers and fathers isn't much better, the national average being about 17 minutes per week(out of a possible 10,080).

Most young people today watch 40 to 60 hours per week of television. To help escape reality, many kids hide their heads in Atari games, Nintendo games, or other such techno-distractions. Technology has given us the ability to reach around the world with a computer hooked into a telephone line. Yet many people have lost the ability to have a family time just one evening per month.

Members of strong families have good communication skills and spend a lot of time talking with each other. Communication builds a sense of belonging and it "greases the wheels" of family involvement. Through our words, listening skills, and actions, we show that we care.

Traditions and values are passed on by family interaction. Fathers can teach sons and daughters hunting and fishing skills. Moms can work with children in the area of building caring and nurturing habits. Through positive interaction, both parents can establish bonds and help build lasting memories.

God's Word certainly points us to continual and ongoing dialogue with our children—especially in regard to the things of God. God Himself said:

> These commandments that I give you today are to be upon your hearts. Impress them on your children. Talk about them when you sit at home and when you walk along the road, when you lie down and when you get up. Tie them as symbols on your hands and bind them on your foreheads. Write them on the door frames of your houses and on your gates. (Deuteronomy 6:6-9)

Are you interacting with your kids, taking every opportunity to encourage them in making the tough decisions of life? We can teach them to love the Lord—which is a process that begins with personal example: "Love the LORD your God with all your heart and with all your soul and with all your strength" (Deuteronomy 6:5).

Spending Time Together

Today we have allowed the tyranny of the urgent to overshadow our families. We suffer from "hurry sickness" in a society where enough is never enough. People who are burnt-out and overstressed become leaders of our communities.

Many well-intended Christians try to become bionic warriors for Christ. Time with family is forsaken for "kingdom priorities."

Never forget that young people spell the word love "T-I-M-E." The time you give your kids is indicative of how much you value them. It can't just be *quality* time. Without *quantity* there is *no quality*. It is like asking a starving man to be satisfied with taking a single bite of filet mignon.

Over a decade ago, I experienced a life-changing event that caused me to reevaluate my priorities. It was nine o'clock in the evening on April 14, 1981. A few hours earlier I had said good-bye to my beautiful wife and twin 11-year-old sons. We embraced on the front porch as I brushed away the warm tears from their bright and shining faces. It was one of the most difficult moments of my life—saying good-bye to the family I loved, not knowing if I would ever see them again.

Later that day I sat in the quietness of a private room at Samuel Merritt Hospital. As I stared at the stark white walls, I pondered the past and my impending ten-hour operation to remove a nonmalignant tumor from my brain stem.

I let the thought of death become my teacher. Several penetrating questions filled my head. Would I live to see another day? Have I provided sufficient love and encouragement to my twin sons during the past 11 years so that they could make it in this complex world? What had I done to help further God's kingdom and traditional family values?

Each of these questions required me to rethink my past priorities. The reality was that for the first seven years of our boys' lives, I had essentially been an absentee father. I had spent too much time worrying about *being* important instead of *doing* what was important. My time with Dan and Tom had been limited to a quality orientation rather than a quantity consideration.

I'm very thankful for a loving wife who countered my deficiencies during these years. I was also fortunate that God in His grace gave our children a wonderful spirit that made parenting joyous.

In the midst of my health ordeal, I came to realize that all my management awards, fishing achievements, and professional accomplishments ultimately meant nothing. I never heard of a dying man wishing he had worked just a little harder. The temporal rewards of our hurried culture have no eternal value or worth. Solomon was right: "It is all vanity and striving after the wind." What *was* important were the traditional, religious values that had eternal consequences for me and my family.

Following a successful surgery, my life finally became focused upon God and family rather than on myself. Sharing God's plan for balanced living and biblical parenting became my passion. Our ministry developed from a desire to help others better understand God's heart for strong, healthy families.

I've continued to take time with my sons—teaching them about God, life, and how to fish and hunt. Some of our greatest memories have been centered around the time we spent "casting and blasting." Dr. James Dobson is right when he says that "some of life's most important moments are spent during moments of leisure."

It is said of James Boswell, the famous biographer of Samuel Johnson, that he often referred to a special day when his father took him fishing. The day was fixed in his adult mind, and he often reflected upon many of the things his father had taught him in the course of their fishing together. After having read about that particular excursion, it occurred to someone much later to check the journal that Boswell's father kept and determine what had been said from the parental perspective about the fishing trip. Turning to that date, the reader found only one sentence: "Gone fishing today with my son; a day wasted."

Too bad that Boswell's father couldn't appreciate the significance of that fishing trip and what it meant to his son. *No day is ever wasted in the life of a father who spends that day with his son.*[2]

I'm reminded of the story about Mary and Martha in Luke 10:38-42:

> As Jesus and his disciples were on their way, he came to a village where a woman named Martha opened her home to him. She had a sister called Mary, who sat at the Lord's feet listening to what he said. But Martha was distracted by all the preparations that had to be made. She came to him and asked, "Lord, don't you care that my sister has left me to do the work by myself? Tell her to help me!"
>
> "Martha, Martha," the Lord answered, "you are worried and upset about many things, but only one thing is needed. Mary has chosen what is better, and it will not be taken away from her. Enjoy the good part."

What was Jesus saying to Martha? He was telling her to not worry about all her preparations and fretting. He called her to not worry about the urgent and the immediate, but to take the time to enjoy fellowship with Him (the good part). What is the good part you are enjoying with your family? Are you choosing what is better?

Commitment to One Another

In Scripture we find this wonderful promise regarding commitment: "Let us not lose heart in doing good, for in due time we shall reap if we do not grow weary. So then, while we have opportunity, let us do good to all men, and especially to those who are of the household of the faith" (Galatians 6:9,10 NASB).

"Doing good" requires, among other things, that we stay committed to the ones we love. Most dictionaries describe commitment as a *pledge* or *obligation*. Commitment means that, after God, our family comes first. Each member of the family is valued and is viewed as precious. The opinions and attitudes of each individual count and are considered important.

Difficult times such as sickness, quarrels, and other trying situations do not destroy their overarching commitment to one another. Strong families are steady and unwavering in their support. It is good to remember that committed families aren't any more righteous or pure than others; they just have ways of dealing with their problems that distinguish them from other families.

Commitment requires sacrifice. It may mean that parents need to sacrifice a certain social or civic involvement in order to keep commitments made to one of the kids. Sacrifice also means that the family doesn't just get the "leftovers" of one's focus and attention. *Stay committed to the cause.* Make your family a top priority. You won't be sorry!

Spiritual Development in the Family

A final trait involves developing a spiritual dimension to your family. The very first institution God created was the family. And it is a spiritual law that the closer each family member is to God, the closer they will subsequently be to each other. Spiritual development in the family, then, is exceedingly important.

Try to turn your kids on to the things of God at an early age (2 Timothy 3:15). And remember, "the religion of a child depends upon what his mother and his father are, and not on what they say." You need to "walk the walk" and not just "talk the talk." Your kids will notice any inconsistencies between what you say and how you live. So make spiritual development a top priority for *all* of your lives.

"As For Me and My Home . . ."

We have fished but only one cove in a vast lake of wisdom and counsel on what the Word of God says about strong families. But there's a final point to make. Paul Overstreet has discovered the truth that Joshua preached to the tribes of Israel almost 4000 years ago: "As for me and my household, we will serve the Lord" (Joshua 24:15). What about your home?

Remember—

... the Christian home is the Master's workshop where the processes of character-molding are silently, lovingly, faithfully, and successfully carried on.

—Richard Monckton Milnes

Personal Growth

• What do you think Moses is teaching us about a strong family life in Deuteronomy 6? Can you find some practical principles for today's family in this passage?

• What are some specific things you can do to encourage the following traits in your family?

Appreciation and encouragement

Good communication

Time together

Commitment

Spiritual development

PERSONAL PROFILE

Paul Overstreet

Background—Born in Mississippi and raised in the South in a single-parent home. Developed musical abilities about the same time he discovered the great outdoors. Is presently one of the top songwriters in the United States. His passion for fishing and hunting is second only to his love of God and family.

Age When First Fish Caught—Four or five years old.

Favorite Bible Verses—Joel 2:25 and Proverbs 22:1.

Family—Married in 1985, five children.

Favorite Fishing Hole—Mountain streams in Idaho.

Favorite Fishing Lure—Rooster Tail.

Preferred Equipment—Spinning.

Most Respected Fishing Pro/Mentor or Instructor—Paul Elias.

Personal Comments—"You need to fight for your family. It requires a dedicated effort to build a strong family. Remember, 'Love Helps Those Who Cannot Help Themselves.'"

14

To Love and to Honor

Fishing with Thomas Kinkade

One of my hobbies is collecting old fishing books. I was recently reading through Fishing Widows, written by Nick Lyons in 1974. His humorous description of fishing is, unfortunately, what many nonfishermen think of when they render an opinion on my favorite sport:

> There is a curious rumor that fishing is idyllic and pastoral, that it rejuvenates the spirit and excites the blood to high adventure, that it requires high intelligence. Here in the city I often dream of idyllic days, when mayflies, tan against a sinking sun, crowd off the water, flutter in clouds down the alley of a stream, and the fish make the surface pocked and choppy with their feeding.
>
> But then I remember: my experience has been otherwise. Your boat leaks. It rains. You fall in, freeze, boil, hook yourself, hook your partner, lose your equipment, catch the weeds, catch pneumonia, snarl your line, get bitten by flies you can't see, miss the big one, and hear, inevitably, that you should have been

there yesterday or last week or next month. If you return alive and sane, no one believes a word you tell them; if you stay out too long or too often, you lose your family or your job. If you don't stay out long enough, he who did will taunt you unto death that "they began to bite like mad ten minutes after you left."

You don't want to neglect your wife, so you take her along: she gets bitten to shreds by black flies and does not speak to you for a year. Not all bad. You take your children along, since you've heard in these hard times the family that fishes together stays together: you spend the day untying knots, the kiddies fall in, you bring them home sopping wet and sneezing, and your wife does not speak to you for another year.

So, why do people fish? Maybe only one man knows. A wise sage, Mr. Edward Zern, claimed that "roughly two-thirds of all fishermen never eat fish. This should surprise nobody. Fish is brain food. People who eat fish have large, well-developed brains. People with large, well-developed brains don't fish."[1]

Lyons has humorously exaggerated the woes of this sport. I would wager a bet (if I were a betting man), however, that if he would develop a relationship with someone who really knows the sport—a real fisherman—he too would discover the many exciting opportunities and challenges that await the converted urbanite.

Such was the case with my friend and internationally known artist, Thomas Kinkade. Thomas grew up in a single-parent home with no dad to teach him about the wonderment and joy found in outdoor activities. Early in his development, his creative energies were consumed with painting and drawing. There were precious few opportunities for him to enjoy the great outdoors in the Sierra foothills of his hometown of Placerville, California.

Using his extremely creative mind, Thomas was able to imagine the outdoor experience that many of his friends talked about. He also visualized a home filled with joy and peace, where shadows of fear, hurt, confusion, and rejection were washed away in a sea of radiant light that comes from Christ-centered love for one another.

Thom's childhood sweetheart, Nanette, shared this vision, and together they agreed to create a real haven for their children. A good, healthy, loving home was a high priority for both of them. "Ever since my wife, Nanette, and I met at age thirteen, we have had a dream of creating a home together—a haven where we could live and raise our children. As our lives have moved forward, we have fought to hold on to that peaceful vision."[2]

Some of the personal traits Thom developed while learning to survive in a dysfunctional home were not advantageous to building a strong marriage. On the one hand, he had the sensitivity and vulnerability that most creative people possess. But deep within was a whole lot of testosterone, driving him to express the masculine side of his personality. Thomas admits that in the first few years of marriage, he had to work on controlling his assertive nature.

"It seemed as if every time I tried to get away from my sensitive nature I would either bowl people over or embarrass myself by acting selfishly," Thomas reflects. "I remember the times I would get upset with Nanette and jump on my big Harley motorcycle in full leathers and run around town acting all macho. After being revived and invigorated, I would return home to have Nanette point out that I had a dab of green paint on the end of my nose. Such experiences helped remind me to be humble."

Another watershed moment in shaping Thom and Nanette's relationship occurred on a fishing trip in Alaska. After a nice breakfast, the two lovebirds climbed into an eight-foot inflatable zodiak with a recently hired guide, who knew as much about fishing as the Kinkades did.

This guide proudly motored her little boat across the inlet to a spot guaranteed to produce fish. Thom sat proudly on the front of the zodiak, peering across the water as if to project his leadership and authority over God's creation.

The two fishing lines were quickly dropped overboard, and just as quickly Thom's rod started dancing around in his hands. "Strike!" the guide shouted.

With all the assurance of a superb fisherman, Thom jerked back and started reeling. "The fish came up pretty easy as I put the pressure on him. The 16-pound halibut swam around the boat a few times before we dumped him into the bottom of the boat. I assured the ladies that my success could be shared with them and that I would show them my technique." Of course, there is no technique in halibut fishing, but neither the women nor Thom knew that. As their eyes rolled around in their heads, Thom cast out again to see if he would be graced with another keeper.

Within minutes Nanette screamed out, "I think I got one—a big one." Her rod tip flexed and the drag began to let out several yards of line. The little boat was pulled around as Nanette struggled to keep the rod in her hands.

The fight was exhausting, and her slender arms began to throb as another hooked halibut swam to the surface. The fish was huge. At four-and-a-half feet it was not much smaller than the bottom of the boat.

Thom seemed to lose his assured, self-reliant attitude and exclaimed, "What do we do now?" The guide was equally baffled as she admitted that this was her first experience fishing out of a small boat. Thom decided the fish needed to be gaffed. So he grabbed the old wooden-handled stick with its rusty hook and struck it into the side of the churning halibut. Everyone helped grab the gaff and pull the flopping fish into the boat.

"The halibut began to break-dance all over the boat and its three occupants," Thomas recalls. "Gear, lunches, cameras, and clothing were flying everywhere. The scene must have looked like the deck of the Titanic as it was sinking."

Everyone realized that Nanette's fish needed more room, and that unless they got rid of it someone was going to get hurt. Thom thought it might be better to bludgeon the fish to death with the hook-end of the gaff. As he raised his arms for the first blow, he realized that they were in ice-cold water in a small inflatable boat that could easily puncture if he should miss the fish.

They unanimously agreed to hoist the fish overboard, with the gaff still in its side, and drag it to the nearest beach. At this point, the three mariners pelted the fish with anything that was available—rocks, cans, suntan lotion, sticks, and, of course, the gaff. Finally, they lifted the dead fish aboard and motored back to the lodge—as victors.

The boat ride back allowed Thom to reflect on his attitude and actions. His macho ego was deflated as he thought about his role as protector, provider, and leader of his wife and family. It would seem that God provided this lesson to help him readjust his thinking to better understand what it means to be a servant-leader. He realized the need to be vulnerable and open with the one he loved most, to work on eliminating pretense and self-reliance, and seek instead to support, counsel, and encourage his mate.

Love Never Fails

Life experiences have taught several invaluable lessons to Thomas Kinkade about loving and honoring his wife. Many of these reflections are shared in his best-selling book *Simpler Times*, published by Harvest House Publishers. The title accurately portrays this man's vision and passion for developing a successful marriage and home for their beautiful children.

Thomas would never claim to be an expert on marriage (and neither would I). I seriously doubt if any man can truly say he has mastered his marriage relationship to perfection. However, both of us are committed to making our marriages a top priority. If we fail to do this, life will inevitably take bites out of our relationship, leaving it scarred with cuts, nicks, and deep wounds.

I am reminded of the great story *The Old Man and the Sea*, by Ernest Hemingway. I am certain that every fisherman has read it and vicariously experienced the pain, struggle, and effort of landing a giant fish. I am also certain that most every man has experienced the pain, struggle, and hard work involved in winning the affections of a certain woman.

Boy, the things we will do to attract a gal! I remember when I was a teenager I rode my broken single-speed bicycle 15 miles just to spend an hour with a girlfriend. I worked nights and Saturdays fitting shoes on stinky feet at a local store so I would have enough money to buy my date perfume, flowers, candy, and anything else I could use to spoil her. From time to time, I even canceled fishing trips with my buddies because I had landed a date with a high school heartthrob. It began to look as if attracting the opposite sex had become my second job.

Like the old man in the story, Thom and I finally landed the beauties we had dreamed of. We both have great marriages to wonderful women. But just as the fisherman, journeying home with his awesome catch, began to see sharks come and take bites out of his prized fish, so I have seen that our marriages can be eaten up by life's pressures. The old fisherman could only watch, as more and more sharks came to take their bites. When it was over, the fish was gone. The old man had only memories and regrets. I will never let my marriage suffer a similar fate.

We men tend to take the marriage relationship we've worked so hard to obtain and troll it behind the boat of life. Small bites of daily commitments, kids activities, church engagements, and work priorities can grab off bits and parts that are needed to sustain a healthy relationship.

I'm reminded of the postcard that reads, "Wanted: A wife to be my fishing partner who has a good boat and friendly dog. Send pictures of the boat and dog." We often forget about our first loves—our wives.

God's Plan for Marriage

I can think of nothing more important than for the men of our nation to turn their hearts back to home—starting with their wives. Did you know that more than 50 percent of our nation's marriages end in divorce? The divorce rate is three times higher than it was in 1962. Violence and spousal abuse are on the rise. In some inner cities over 80 percent of families do not have a male role model in the home. Families are under attack as never before. Broken homes start with broken marriages. If we truly endeavor to better understand our wives and our responsibilities associated with marriage, we can begin to build lasting marriages and stronger homes.

Despite all the great psychology and profound thoughts of man on the topic of marriage, in what follows I will turn to the most reliable source for guidance—the Bible, God's Word. Consider these three basic biblical principles:

1. *Marriage requires mutual unselfishness*: Scripture says, "Marriage is not a place to 'stand up for your rights.' Marriage is a decision to serve the other" (1 Corinthians 7:4, THE MESSAGE).

The apostle Paul also instructs,

Husbands, go all out in your love for your wives, exactly as Christ did for the church—a love marked by giving, not getting. Christ's love makes the church whole. His words evoke her beauty. Everything he does and says is designed to bring the best out of her, dressing her in dazzling white silk, radiant with holiness. And that is how husbands ought to love their wives (Ephesians 5:25, THE MESSAGE).

2. *Marriage includes times of testing and trials*: When Paul, a single man, addressed people who had a desire to get married, he warned them that "such will have trouble in this life, and I am trying to spare you" (1 Corinthians 7:26 THE MESSAGE). He later writes, "Sometimes I wish everyone were single like me—a simpler life in many ways!" (1 Corinthians 7:28, THE MESSAGE). This is not to dissuade anyone from getting married. It is simply to point out that there will be trials in any marriage relationship.

3. *Marriage means lifelong commitment.* Paul said, "But to the married I give instructions, not I, but the Lord, that the wife should not leave her husband . . . and that the husband should not send his wife away" (1 Corinthians 7:10-12 NASB). In 1 Peter 3:5 we are likewise instructed, "Be good husbands to your wives. Honor them, delight in them" (THE MESSAGE).

As I ponder these points, it strikes me that fishermen spend countless hours selecting, sorting, restoring, and polishing lures, reels, rods, and other assorted gear. It's great fun. We do all this so we can woo some unsuspecting fish into taking our offerings. We would never think of using just one plug. We remain versatile in our approach and fresh in our understanding so we can have the best chance of influencing the fish to bite.

Marriage is no different. We need to spend time on the little things that allow for a successful marriage. We need to sharpen the hooks of forgiveness, polish the spoons of tenderness, and sort through the challenges and opportunities that give hope to the future.

Also, let's not approach the pond of lovemaking with the same old standard cast in the same old way. If a fish can get "turned off" with a stale presentation, so can a wife. Be creative, exciting, and imaginative—your "fishing" will never be the same.

Loving Another

Counselor H. Norman Wright compiled a number of warm and tender thoughts in a small book called *Quiet Moments for Couples*. Let me close with three thoughts he cited on what it means to love another:

- Love is a long conversation where each tells by gentle words, by glances, by thoughtful deeds, and unexpected kindness, that you care, that you understand, that you will be true.

- Love is expressed unmistakably with the eyes. In giving attention, we give affection . . . Love is expressed undeniably with the ears. In hearing another's true intentions we give affection.

- Love is expressed unequivocally in . . . the availability offered. The assurance that each will be there for the other when needed, when expected, when desired, is the confidence of being loved.[3]

Personal Growth

- What does it mean to honor your wife? Does Ephesians 5 help you to understand God's plan for marriage?

- What are five practical things you can do so your wife will feel understood and honored?

    a.

    b.

    c.

    d.

    e.

PERSONAL PROFILE

Thomas Kinkade

Thomas has traveled the United States and seen the world from a "hobo's" eyes. After studying with several artists, Thomas developed the style and grace that sets his beautiful artwork apart. He is the acclaimed "Painter of Light," and has received numerous national awards for his work, including the 1994 Lithograph of the Year Award and 1995 Artist of the Year. He rides a big motorcycle and swims with his three daughters.

Background—Raised by his mother in Placerville, California.

Age When First Fish Caught—Seven years old (a two-and-a-half-inch fish caught out of Lumson's Pond).

Favorite Bible Verse—Psalm 119:105.

Family—Married to Nanette. Three beautiful girls.

Favorite Fishing Hole—Delta.

Favorite Fishing Lure—Green Grub.

Preferred Equipment—Spinning-Fly Fishing.

Most Respected Fishing Pro/Mentor or Instructor—Bel Lange.

Personal Comments—"Painter of Light" is more than a marketing term. "Paintings usually are a permanent feature in a home or office constantly bringing a message to folks. I want to be sure that my work is inspired by God and brings joy and encouragement to help point people to Christ."

15

Encouraging Others

Fishing with Jack Arthur

Jack knew that if he finished all his chores, granddad would take him down to the nearby Big Walnut River for another fishing lesson. His grandfather was a hard-working farmer whose values and efforts served as a great model for young Jack.

Growing up as a child without a mom or dad was uncommon back in the 1930s. Jack's mother had never married the man who forced his intentions upon her. The result was a pregnancy that fortunately was not terminated.

Jack was raised with plenty of encouragement, partly because his grandparents knew there would be many difficult times ahead for him. Participating in sports was not a big part of Jack's life, but the lure of the river and the challenge of the fish were very inspiring to him.

His grandparents were his "balcony people"—his *rooters*. They considered every chance they got to inspire Jack with hope and assurance an opportunity to invest in his life. Grandma would often accompany him down to the river with a big picnic basket filled with fried chicken and goodies that nurtured his body, while her quiet but penetrating words of comfort and assurance helped paint a positive future for him. His grandparents subscribed to the philosophy, "Don't forget that a pat on the back can cause a chin to go up and shoulders to go back."[1]

At 26 years of age, Jack dedicated himself to Jesus Christ and began to apply the encouragement of his new faith to daily living. This was about the time he became acquainted with Jim Heaton, another avid fisherman. Their mutual appreciation for one another quickly created the framework for a lifetime friendship.

Jim and Jack have taken many wonderful fishing trips together. But none was more memorable than their trip to the Cooks Inlet in Alaska in 1985. It would be their third trip to this pristine wonderland.

They had enjoyed several days of good fishing during the infamous "king salmon run." It was a calm morning with fair weather when Jim and Jack jumped on-board the small fishing boat skippered by the seasoned guide, Mike Chihuly. They began trolling out of the marina when Jim's reel suddenly started singing. A huge king salmon took his spoon and was heading to deeper water. Jack reeled in his line and began cheering for Jim, just the way his grandmother used to root for him. The fight went on for minutes when, finally, Mike slipped the big net under the salmon and hoisted him aboard. After several "high fives," they measured the fish off at 58 pounds.

They placed the lines back into the water as the engines once again began their monotonous groan. Jack told Jim that his salmon looked "very lonely in the fish box—perhaps he needed some company."

Suddenly Jack's Garcia-7000 reel began to sing out. The skipper stopped the boat and directed Jack to set the hook. As he lifted the rod, the butt section dug into his gut and the tip bent down to the gunwale. The monster salmon began to tail-walk across the water as if to tease the helpless anglers. There was no way they were going to stop this weighty fish with 30-pound test line on a medium-weight rod.

As Jack gazed at his reel, the silver shine of the metal spool began to peek through the remaining monofilament line. Mike shouted, "If we're going to have any chance of getting this fish, we're going to have to chase him." *And chase they did.* Mike began motoring toward the fish at about ten miles per hour while Jack was reeling as fast as he could.

The smiles of the crew and shouts of glee suddenly turned to despair. Jack was not gaining anything on the fish. His old reel had not survived the initial run and had experienced a "meltdown"—the hot gears froze up.

The fish continued its surge as it led the perplexed anglers through a maze of boats and other anglers' lines. One by one, the onlooking anglers either reeled in their lines or cut their rigs to give Jack a chance of landing his trophy. About the time Jack was ready to throw his rod and reel overboard, he heard shouts of inspiration coming from many of the onlookers: "Hang in there!" "Keep on battling!" "You're whipping 'um!"

Mike suggested that Jack empty the line off his battered reel and retie his line onto Jim's reel once he removed all his existing line. What seemed like an eternity was in reality only a few minutes. Jim directed Jack to grab hold of the line while Mike tried to keep moving with the fish. This gave Jim an opportunity to quickly tie Jack's line to the working reel and place it on the rod.

The stinging spray from the mist of saltwater, mixed with beads of perspiration, flowed into Jack's eyes as he and Jim struggled with the gear. Jim's hands were shaking so much with excitement that he could barely tie a good knot to the empty reel. Things weren't going well.

But at least now, Jack could begin to place some real pressure on the fish. Just as he had encouraged Jim earlier, it was now Jim's turn to encourage Jack to persevere and keep a positive outlook. Every time Jack said he wasn't going to land the fish, Jim was there to remind him of God's faithfulness, and that with patience, he would be the victor.

It was now about 45 minutes into the fight when, finally, the tired salmon turned on its side. Jim and Mike took the net and slid the front half of the 57.5-inch giant as far as it would go. Then, on the count of three, they lifted the net into the bottom of the boat. The big salmon seemed to gaze at the weary fishermen as if to admit its own defeat.

This 85-pound salmon is still ranked number one in the world in the open saltwater class and is ranked in the top ten salmon ever caught on a hook and line. Today it is stuffed and hangs in Jack's office as a constant reminder of what encouragement means.

Encouragement Is Infectious

Encouragement is often neglected in our self-centered culture. The "me generation" places more emphasis on individualism than on teamwork. As Christians, however, we are instructed to encourage one another. Larry Crabb, Jr. and Dan Allender, in their outstanding book *Encouragement*, write:

> Christians are commanded to encourage one another. Because words have the power to affect people deeply, it is appropriate to consider how to encourage fellow Christians through what we say. Words can encourage, discourage, or do nothing. We must learn to speak sincerely with positive impact, using our words to help other Christians pursue the pathway of obedience more zealously.[2]

The act of inspiring others should be a regular part of our Christian lives. There are many lessons on encouragement in Scripture—but probably none more powerful than two from our Savior's life.

On two separate occasions God the Father chose to publicly commend, inspire, and encourage Jesus. As an assembled crowd looked on, John the Baptist blessed and baptized Jesus in the Jordan River. God the Father appreciated the moment and the willingness of Christ to apply Himself to the call. The Father openly proclaimed, "This is My beloved Son, in whom I am well pleased" (Matthew 3:17 NASB). And again, the same supporting message was proclaimed at the end of His ministry: "This is My beloved Son, with whom I am well-pleased; listen to Him!" (Matthew 17:5 NASB).

What was the Father saying? It appears that these chosen words were intended to convey His total support, approval, and love of Jesus. Wasn't He really saying, "I love you! I'm proud of you! You're okay!"?

The Purpose of Christ's Ministry

When we consider the various Scriptures that could have been used to announce Jesus' impending ministry, He chose the book of Isaiah to emphasize not only His work as Savior but also the importance of encouragement. Shortly after returning from Galilee "in the power of the Spirit," He began His teaching ministry at a synagogue in His hometown of Nazareth. He declared His mission and purpose this way:

> The Spirit of the Lord is on me, because he has anointed me to preach good news to the poor. He has sent me to proclaim freedom for the prisoners and recovery of sight for the blind, to release the oppressed, to proclaim the year of the Lord's favor (Luke 4:18-19).

Jesus was essentially saying, "I'm here to save you, as well as to inspire, support, lift up, and encourage you." We all need encouragers, exhorters, coaches, and helpers—people who sit in the balcony and root us on. Through the written Word and the guidance of the Holy Spirit, Jesus can provide that ultimate inspiration and support that is so vital to fueling the motivation and stimulation we need to live a creative life in Christ.

We all *need* encouragers and we should all *be* encouragers to others. The apostle Paul provides an excellent example of both. He received encouragement from a peer supporter—Barnabas. This exhorter emerged from the Island of Cyprus and took on Paul as a primary disciple. There are those who would say that Barnabas was the "minister of encouragement," and, in fact, his name actually means "son of encouragement" (Acts 4:36). The lessons learned from Barnabas helped stimulate Paul's inspirational ministry and his subsequent mentoring of many others.

Jack Arthur was able to land the salmon that memorable day and become an inspirational leader largely because his grandparents and caring friends had modeled encouragement. Do you want to be successful? Would you like a strong marriage and home? Are you interested in building a successful church? The first step is to become an encourager!

How Peter Became an Encourager

In *Promising Waters: Stories of Fishing and Following Jesus,* I take a close look at the relationship Jesus had with His disciples. His encouraging ways inspired and motivated these men to propel a ministry into the ages.

Fishermen by their nature tend to be optimistic. We think that every cast or throw of the net will produce fish. We look at every day and every fishing hole as an opportunity to learn more about our favorite sport. Yet, even with all our optimism, we sometimes feel the despair of failure and defeat. The fish seem to have more victories than we do. Fishermen have greater "highs" and lower "lows" than most athletes. Despite our skill, much of our success depends on something we really can't control—the bite.

All this reminds me of what we might call "Murphy's Laws for Angling":

• When conditions are supposed to be just right,
  they won't be.

- The number of fish caught by an angler is inversely proportionate to how much he or she deserves it.

- When a fish falls off the hook and lands on the gunwale, it will bounce overboard 99 percent of the time.

- The more money you spend on a fly rod, the more likely you are to break the tip in your car door jam.

- If you have six lines in the water, the biggest fish of the day will always hit the one with a nick on it.

- The biggest fish of the day will always hit the lightest line.

- The angler that brags the most catches the fewest fish.

- Where the fish were biting yesterday, they won't today.

I'm sure Peter would have identified with these "laws." Certainly his life was like a seesaw of ups and downs. Despite his struggles, though, Peter learned a great deal about encouragement from his relationship with Jesus. The book of Acts describes the encouraging influence that Peter himself subsequently had on the fledgling church at Pentecost. He inspired and fostered spiritual growth in each person he connected with.

Peter learned to encourage others as a result of the encouragement he received from Jesus. Many scholars believe that Jesus lived with Peter and his family for two of His three-and-one-half years of ministry. Jesus could relate to Peter and His family in a special way. He knew that encouragement must start at home. He knew His time was limited and that He needed to build a strong, supportive relationship with each of His disciples.

There was an intimacy between Jesus and the disciples that suggests a deep respect and admiration. Jesus called each of them to that depth of commitment and relationship when He said, "follow Me." Without a pledge of commitment, an encourager cannot be effective. The relationship must first be built before encouragement can take place.

The same thing is true in our own families. We can become an encourager to our families—especially to our kids—if we first take the time and effort necessary to build those relationships. I'm convinced that if every home had a committed and encouraging father, we could lessen our worry about gangs, suicides, drugs, teen pregnancy, and a host of other ills that plague our youth.

Just take a look at what we're up against. In general, our culture is anything but encouraging. The media tells us that if we don't buy the right products, we can't expect to smell good, have friends, keep our hair, and the like. The direct and indirect messages are "You're a loser" and "I'm better than you."

Life can get especially discouraging for our young people. Psychologists tell us that a child needs ten positive affirmations for every negative message he or she receives.

One of my favorite stories about encouraging family members comes from quarterback Bart Starr. In 1965 this Green Bay Packer was encouraging his team to a championship. Bart was known to be an encourager to his team and especially to his son—Bart, Jr. His son needed large doses of encouragement because of problems he faced resulting from peer group pressures.

Bart couldn't spend much time with his family, but he kept plugged into their lives. His wife would often leave some of Junior's school papers on the kitchen table for his review when he came in late at night. Bart would praise Junior with notes of encouragement—"I love you and I'm proud of you"—with a dime taped to the paper. This was a tremendous encouragement to young Bart.

During the season, Bart, Sr. once had a very difficult day while playing against St. Louis. He was intercepted several times and fumbled the ball during the last possession. This cost his team the victory. The long plane ride back home was dreary.

Bart entered his home late that night to find a note on the kitchen table. It read: "I watched the game today. I believe you are still #1. I love you—and I'm proud of you." What an encouragement to a discouraged dad!

We are called to uplift one another. Regardless of our circumstances, may we continue to be strong and consistent encouragers—especially to family members. The opposite is also true: no matter what age, dads also need the encouragement of their families. In fact, I believe that a successful and truly fulfilled man can be measured by the encouragement he receives from his family.

Encouraging Truths to Live By

Look to the Future

Jack Arthur's grandparents provided him with a positive vision toward his future that stimulated creativity and exhorted him to action. The daily words and acts of kindness that were woven into the fabric of his life became a beautiful tapestry of commitment and service. What patterns and design are you imprinting onto the fabric of your own children's lives?

Jesus is the ultimate encourager because He looks to the future and forgives the past. Christ's focus with Peter was not where this Galilean fisherman had been, but where he was going—it involved a vision not of what he was, but of what he would become.

Consider the occasion when Jesus first met Peter: "Jesus looked at him and said, 'You are Simon son of John. You will be called Cephas' (which, when translated, is Peter)" (John 1:42). Jesus looked deep within Peter to his very soul. He pointed to Peter's *future*—that of being part of the foundation for the first century church. Our Savior could see Peter's potential, and Peter did in fact assume a leadership role after Pentecost.

How important is this "perspective of encouragement" to how we relate to others? *It is everything.* If people sense a genuine encouragement and support for their future longings and dreams, they can be motivated to give their very best.

Gary Smalley and John Trent believe this is so critical that they devoted a significant part of their book, *The Blessing*, to this concept as related to raising children.

> Words that picture a special future act like a campfire on a dark night. They can draw a person toward the warmth of genuine concern and fulfilled potential. Instead of leaving a child to head into a dark unknown, they can illuminate a pathway lined with hope and purpose.[3]

People will respond to our expectations. If we project a negative, discouraging future, people usually respond in kind. Folks who are encouragers often witness considerable growth and commitment in individuals who are motivated by inspirational acts.

Fortunately for my wife and me, we received a word from God on this concept when we were young parents. Our boys were given the rich gift of music from God when they were six years of age. Louise and I endeavored to support them in their gift and tried to paint a bright future as related to their unique ability. While there are some things we might change in the way we parented our children, this area of our support was, we believe, hopefully significant.

Encouragement Will Stretch and Grow People

Over 20 years ago, Kay and Jack Arthur started meeting with small groups, and many folks encouraged them in this start-up ministry. Jack could see the calling of his wife, Kay, and how people responded to her teaching. He realized that his gift and calling was to be inspiring and supportive of her work.

Precept by precept, and with the grace of God, Kay and Jack Arthur built an international ministry. Their Precepts Ministry has more than 6000 classes meeting weekly with 22 different study manuals. Kay is a best-selling author of 16 books with radio and television programs that have inspired hundreds of thousands of people.

Jack was always there to encourage Kay as she stretched and grew in her vision for this Bible study ministry. He is a great model of how and why we should be supportive to people when they are seeking to fulfill a dream.

On many occasions, Jack has been stretched to consider new and different challenges. The salmon fishing trip was one example of how he would be challenged in his faith and perseverance. As new opportunities have arisen, Jack and Kay have expanded their ministry as they've ventured through uncharted waters.

Jesus encouraged Peter to new experiences. He inspired him to stretch and grow, even in the midst of his failures. We must not forget that failure is an acceptable, albeit temporary, by-product of personal and spiritual growth. The essence of our Christian faith allows for forgiveness and unlimited second chances.

Peter was no exception. Jesus could have informed him that he would fail many more times than he would succeed. He could have told him that he would sink in the water because his faith was too weak. But He didn't!

When the disciples saw him walking on the lake, they were terrified. "It's a ghost," they said, and cried out in fear.

> But Jesus immediately said to them, "Take courage! It is I. Don't be afraid."
>
> "Lord, if it's you," Peter replied, "tell me to come to you on the water."
>
> "Come," he said.
>
> Then Peter got down out of the boat, walked on the water and came toward Jesus (Matthew 14:26-29).

When people take risks—*when they are stretching*—stay with them. Be ready to offer your support. Sometimes encouragement takes the form of being a safety net, catching others after a fall. Oftentimes silence is the best encouragement. It isn't always words that encourage, but a warm smile, a firm handshake, an embracing hug, or smiling eyes.

Never Abandon Others

Jack's grandparents chose to lend him a helping hand. They stuck with him through the tough times. Abandonment wasn't an option.

The up-and-down life of Peter can be seen time and time again in the New Testament. In Matthew 16:18, for example, Jesus affirmed Peter as the "rock," only to rebuke him a little later for being a stumbling block (see verses 21-23). Then Peter denied Christ three times before the crucifixion (Matthew 26:69-75)!

Despite Peter's failures, Jesus continued to support him. At the end of His ministry on earth, Jesus asked Peter to reaffirm his love, and then promptly encouraged him and the other disciples in their future ministries.

We will all stumble and fall short from time to time. We will fail one another and God. Jesus did not abandon His disciples when they failed but rather remained supportive and faithful. He never gave up on them, even at the cross.

Neither will our Lord ever give up on you or me. He sent the Holy Spirit to minister to us and to be the ultimate supporter, comforter, and encourager (John 14:16). He also regularly intercedes with the Father on our behalf (Hebrews 7:25).

Who are the people you are thinking about giving up on? Remember, a committed encourager will exhaust all resources while continuing to try and motivate others. Jesus reached out to Peter as he was sinking. He didn't let him go under. Encouragers need to regularly reach out to others and help pull them up.

One of the best ways to help uplift individuals is to become a prayer warrior for those you wish to inspire. Prayer is powerful and will help unleash the power of God in their lives. Someone said, "A friend will strengthen you with his prayers, bless you with his love, and encourage you with his hope."

Personal Growth

• What are some ways you can be an exhorter to others? Read the following for some insights on this:

> Romans 15:4-9
>
> 1 Thessalonians 5:11
>
> 2 Timothy 4:2
>
> Colossians 2:1-2
>
> Philemon 1:7

• What kind of model for encouragement does Jesus demonstrate in Mark 10:13-16?

• Discuss Jesus' encouragement of Peter with a friend. Center the discussion on the following points:

1. Focus on the potential in others, not on past failures (John 1:40-42).

2. Help others when they are in a process of growth (Matthew 14:26-31).

3. Never give up on the relationship (Matthew 16).

PERSONAL PROFILE

Jack Arthur

Background—Raised in Indiana by his grandparents. Has loved to fish all his life. Serves as president of Precept Ministry.

Age When First Fish Caught—Five or six years old.

Favorite Bible Verses—Philippians 4:19 and Psalm 91:2.

Family—Wife, Kay (Bible teacher/author), three children, eight grandchildren.

Favorite Fishing Hole—Ninilchik, Alaska.

Favorite Fishing Lure—Silver Rattletrap.

Preferred Equipment—Spinning.

Most Respected Fishing Pro/Mentor or Instructor—Jimmy Houston.

Personal Comments— "Encourage one another!"

Discovering and Using
Your Spiritual Gifts

Fishing with Al Lindner

Shortly after graduating from high school, Al Lindner and his brother Ron began a quest for knowledge and fishing that continues even today. As they toured the northeastern states, the two Lindner boys invested all they had in buying fishing and marine equipment. They used this equipment to challenge local anglers to fishing derbies.

They were among the first to purchase a Lowrance Sonar Unit (little green box). Understanding topography and its impact on structure-fishing was the advantage these talented men needed to beat local pros on their own water.

During the course of events, Al ran into Bill Binkelman, publisher and editor of *Fishing Facts* magazine. While most outdoor magazines were long on experiential stories and general product information, Bill had developed a journal that was scientifically based. He decided to take on a mentoring role with Al.

Bill reminded Al that he had a special gift for fishing—a gift and ability that he had seen in only a few people. It became apparent that this gift was truly an inspired talent for fishing, as he continued to match his abilities and knowledge with some of the nation's best anglers.

In the early 1970s the Lindner brothers developed a plastic worm company that utilized the latest technology and scientific concepts. The Lindy Tackle Company soon became as famous as the Lindners.

It was a late summer afternoon when the telephone rang and the gravelly voice of Virgil Ward asked to speak with Al. For years Al had admired the legendary angler and his nationally syndicated fishing television show. Virgil was on one of his filming trips in the Minnesota area and was striking out on finding any walleyes. He asked Al if he knew of any good spots, and requested assistance in locating the fish.

Al was only too happy to oblige. They agreed to meet the following morning at a small local lake—South Long Lake.

The Bass Buster jigs Al brought along were just becoming popular and the resident walleye seemed to welcome the slow-moving baits. Al convinced Virgil that these fish had never seen an artificial lure. This lure, along with the sonar unit Al used to locate the fish, proved to be a winning combination.

The camera started rolling and the fish started biting. "The day was spectacular," Al recalls. "Everything seemed to work. Virgil caught several nice-sized walleye and had enough footage to do a couple of shows."

Al discovered that making a video was extremely challenging but very rewarding. He realized that a person could combine a scientific approach with a little showmanship and develop a product that could help educate and encourage other fishermen.

The next day Al shared his thoughts with Ron. They agreed that developing a local fishing program and magazine would help stimulate sales for their budding tackle company. That day they went out and purchased a camera and started shooting fishing videos.

The little fishing trip with Virgil Ward launched the In-Fisherman Network, which is now the largest fishing communications organization in the world. Today In-Fisherman boasts of 800 radio stations, a 52-week television program with four camera crews, six different magazines with a total subscription of over 500,000 readers, videos, books, consulting services, and 56 full-time employees.

In 1980 Al joined the rest of his family by dedicating his life to the Lord Jesus Christ. The story of his conversion can be found in my book *Promising Waters*. Shortly after Al's conversion, he and his partner-brother dedicated the entire business to the Lord. Every publication, video, and television program they produce either begins or ends with the "ichthys" superimposed on a cross. This is a symbol for all to see that the company is dedicated to God, and that any success it enjoys is directly related to the God-given abilities and gifts of the staff.

Every Person Unique

Strong forces are at work in our culture that foster feelings of low self-esteem in many of us. These feelings are not uncommon even among persons with significant ego strength. To some individuals, poor self-image can become debilitating, lessening their impact on family, church, and community.

Christ came to reveal God's infinite love and grace for His finite creation. Every person is wonderfully crafted so that no two are exactly alike. The very gift of our personhood is a fundamental aspect of our giftedness. A disciple is called to fulfill his or her potential and utilize all God-given gifts and talents in serving Him.

The average person doesn't consider him- or herself as being gifted. After all, it's really only the top one-tenth of one percent of people in any particular discipline who are truly gifted. We look at capable folks who are extremely visible such as Billy Graham, Reggie White, Roy Rogers, Pat Boone, Rosey Grier, Wayne Watson, and Kathy Lee Gifford, all of whom have obvious skills. By comparison, some of us may be tempted to think less of our own gifts than we should.

The fact is, we are all given a *unique* blend of attitudes, temperaments, talents, natural skills, and abilities that affect our spiritual passion for service. All of this is what makes us uncommon.

We read in 1 Corinthians 12:1-11 that God has blessed believers with a great variety of gifts. Each disciple is given one or more gifts to encourage and serve the church—other believers (Ephesians 4:11-13). Every Christian has a part to play in the effective working of the church (verse 16). The potential for blessing others can be seen as we leaf through Scripture— especially 1 Corinthians 12:1-11, Ephesians 4:11-13, 1 Peter 4:10-11, Romans 12:6-8, and Galatians 5. (I encourage you to look up these passages.)

Because some of the people in the city of Corinth misused their gifts, the apostle Paul felt it necessary to warn the new believers that a spiritual gift is totally ineffective to achieve its intended purpose unless the expression of that gift is motivated by love. The purest form of expression of any gift is when it is expressed with a heart of love and sacrifice towards another person. We should periodically ask ourselves, Am I using my gifts to honor and glorify God, and to uplift other disciples?

The spiritual gifts that are provided to us by God are not to be confused with natural talents and personality traits. Spiritual gifts are not taught or selected. They are given to us by the Holy Spirit (1 Corinthians 12:11) and noticed and affirmed by others. Confirmation of your spiritual gift(s) should be sought from trusted, mature leaders who know you.[1]

Dr. Jon McNeff, of the Evangelical Free Church of Walnut Creek, California, developed a wonderful spiritual gift inventory entitled *Power Tools*. The following definitions and explanations from Jon's booklet will enable you to get a good handle on the specific gift(s) God has given you.[2]

SPIRITUAL GIFT INVENTORY

SERVING GIFTS
Serving
Mercy
Exhortation
Giving

COMMUNICATION GIFTS
Prophecy
Teaching

STUDY GIFTS
Knowledge
Discernment
Wisdom

MINISTRY GIFTS
Evangelism
Pastor

LEADERSHIP GIFTS
Leadership
Administration
Faith

Serving Gifts

1. The Gift of Service (Romans 12:7)

The gift of service involves physical help or relief that is given in a supportive role, usually in a temporary capacity. One who serves does so with joy, and does so whenever necessary to free someone else up for his or her ministry. In Romans 12:7 the word used is *diakonos,* which gave rise to the English word *deacon.* Most feel that the same gift is seen in 1 Corinthians 12:28 where the word *helper* literally means "to take a burden on oneself in place of another." This gift might be exercised today in setting up tables for banquets, working in the nursery, helping on building maintenance, assisting with office clerical work, helping a friend with yard work, helping a child with studies, or perhaps running an errand for a friend.

2. The Gift of Mercy (Romans 12:8)

The gift of mercy involves compassionately and joyfully seeking to alleviate someone's suffering. More than pity, the word *mercy* conveys the idea of benefit that is the result of compassion. It is directed toward the outcast, the poor, the underprivileged, the ill, the deprived, the handicapped, and the retarded. We see an example of this gift in 2 Timothy 1:16-18.

This gift is evidenced not by a long face that adds to the afflicted person's self-pity, but by cheerful encouragement and service. The gift of mercy can be exercised in hospitals, convalescent homes, jails, or in a church ministry with those who are ill. It can also be used in connection with drug addicts, alcoholics, transients, unwed mothers, and single parents.

3. The Gift of Exhortation (Romans 12:8)

The gift of exhortation involves practical and verbal encouragement that is offered as a help and a comfort. The one gifted with exhortation does not resort to verbal brow-beating but instead is one who is "called alongside of" to help or comfort someone. In reality this may be called the gift of *encouragement*. This person is a good listener, derives joy from cheering up people, and can empathize with others' needs without themselves being dragged down.

This gift is evidenced in Paul's attitude toward the beloved Thessalonian church (1 Thessalonians 2:10-12). One who is gifted in exhortation will not be blind to the reality of a bad situation, but will sensibly evaluate and lovingly guide and encourage the people involved. This gift may be exercised by taking someone out to lunch that needs encouragement, by being positive when someone approaches you with a problem, and by generally being sensitive to people's needs.

4. The Gift of Giving (Romans 12:8)

The gift of giving involves the ability and willingness to respond liberally to someone's need without any thought of repayment. This gift is used to supply the needs of others who are unable to do so. It can involve the giving of anything material, or time, or of one's self. The gift has nothing to do with how many material possessions one has but is rather driven by the thrill of being able to help another person. Mark 12:41-42 depicts the poor widow using this gift.

The gift of giving can be exercised by donating money to special projects, cheerfully loaning one's car for youth sponsors to use in transportation, giving food, clothing, shelter, or money to those who need it, or giving oneself and one's time to a friend. It may also be used to help a student in financial need or in response to a specific missions need.

Study Gifts

5. The Gift of Knowledge (1 Corinthians 12:8)

The gift of knowledge involves the ability to study and grasp the mystery of God's revelation and apply it to contemporary life. Knowledge is the gift of desiring to gather all the available pertinent material on a given subject. In short, the one who has this gift enjoys studying and has an insatiable desire to know.

The one who "work[s] hard at preaching and teaching" (1 Timothy 5:17 NASB) will be one who spends time seeking to discover what all the available resources say about an issue. Knowledge involves the assimilation of the facts of unchanging truth that are gained through teaching and written sources, which is then applied to contemporary, changing situations. It does not involve an ethereal vision or instantaneous revelation of new truth. One who claims divine revelation is a deceiver and contradicts God's revealed Word (Revelation 22:18; Jude 3; 1 Corinthians 14:37-38). This gift is exercised in teaching, writing, and effective biblical counseling.

6. The Gift of Discernment (1 Corinthians 12:10)

The gift of discernment involves the ability to separate, examine, and judge spiritual issues to determine which are from God and which are from Satan. It involves the discerning of the spiritual origin of a message. All Christians are to do this (1 John 4:1), but not everyone will have the same ability to do so.

For everything that God has, Satan has a counterfeit. It is therefore important to be able to tell the difference. Some will be in the church (Acts 20:29-30) speaking "in the name of Jesus," but not all will really be of Him. Paul discerned this in Acts 16:16-18. One can apply this to pastors, teachers, friends, and people who claim they've received a revelation from God. One who has the gift of discernment will *know Scripture* and thus be able to "test the spirit" of a teacher (or anyone who says they are from God) and be able to know if they are true or false (1 John 4:1).

7. The Gift of Wisdom (1 Corinthians 12:8)

The gift of wisdom involves the application of God's eternal perspectives to the specific situations in life. Solomon exhibited this ability in 1 Kings 3:23-27.

This gift may be applied in clarifying problems and suggesting solutions, and in being able to reduce biblical truths down to principles for living (like Solomon did in the book of Proverbs). The gift is not necessarily tied to the gift of knowledge, a high IQ, or educational background. It involves the ability to see things as God sees them and bring His truth to bear on the myriad of human situations. It is needed in leadership positions, in counseling situations, and in planning for the future.

Communication Gifts

8. The Gift of Prophecy (Romans 12:6)

The gift of prophecy involves the public proclamation of God's Word that brings conviction for the nonbeliever and encouragement for the believer. Today this is usually associated with preaching. Prophetic preaching that results in conviction of nonbelievers (1 Corinthians 14:25) and the building up, encouragement, and comfort of the saints (1 Corinthians 14:3) stands in the tradition of the Old Testament prophets.

A prophet in biblical times stood in God's place before His people. He was active in both *forthtelling* and *foretelling*. No one today fills the biblical role of prophet completely because no one speaks according to the biblical standards for forthtelling (requiring 100 percent accuracy, according to Deuteronomy 18:20-22), and because no one receives direct revelation from God. (We don't need it in view of the fact that we have the Bible—1 Corinthians 14:27.) But to the extent that one proclaims the Word of God, they may be said to exercise the gift of prophecy when they proclaim "Thus saith the Lord" from the Word of God.

9. The Gift of Teaching (Romans 12:7; 1 Corinthians 12:28; Ephesians 4:11)

The gift of teaching involves the ability to study, grasp, interpret, and communicate the truth of the Word of God effectively. Teaching involves not only the ability to study and grasp (like the gift of knowledge), but also to interpret and explain biblical truths in an understandable way. One who is gifted in this area will have both clear biblical knowledge *and* the ability to apply this knowledge to everyday situations. This person finds it easy to explain things to people.

Second Timothy 2:2 and 3:10 indicate that this gift is exercised not only by word but by one's total way of life. The gift of teaching can be exercised in individual counseling situations, in small interaction groups, and in front of larger groups. It involves not so much the ability to tell people how to swim with diagrams and charts (for example), but to teach them how by getting into the pool with them.

Ministry Gifts

10. The Gift of Evangelism (Ephesians 4:11)

The gift of evangelism involves a special ability to communicate the gospel to a receptive heart and then guide that person into discipleship and the life of a local church. The word *evangelize* literally means "to proclaim good news." The noun form of the word is used only three times in the New Testament where it was seen first as a missionary and then a church-planting gift.

Philip is an example of one who "went where Christ was not named" and led people to Christ (Acts 8:26-40). Timothy also did the work of an evangelist through a more prolonged ministry of teaching aimed at counteracting false teachers (2 Timothy 4:5).

As such, the gift today is not that of the revivalist going from church to church in an attempt to stir up the saints. Nor does it refer to the proverbial "scalphunter." It is most closely seen in the person who can communicate the gospel effectively—*with results*—and then lead that person into the life of a church. The tie to the life of a church is seen in the instruction given to Timothy as a pastor in 1 Timothy 4 and the statement in Ephesians 4:11-12 that the gifts mentioned there were given for the "building up of the body of Christ."

11. The Gift of Pastor (Ephesians 4:11)

The gift of pastor involves a leader who shepherds the flock of God primarily through the teaching of sound doctrine. Since the canon was not closed in the early church, and because books were few and terribly expensive, the role of the pastor as teacher was critical. The teaching shepherd stands against the pagan thought of the day and protects the flock by teaching them that which is food for their souls.

Bible scholar William Barclay comments that the shepherd of the flock of God is "the man who bears God's people on his heart, who feeds them with the truth, who seeks them when they stray away, and who defends them from all that would hurt their faith."[3] The one gifted as pastor will help determine church polity (Acts 15:22), counter pagan thought (Titus 1:9), monitor and lead the activities of the church (Acts 20:28; 1 Timothy 5:17), teach and preach (1 Timothy 3:2), and set an example (1 Peter 5:1-3).

Leadership Gifts

11. The Gift of Leadership (Romans 12:8)

The gift of leadership involves the ability to mobilize, motivate, and direct others toward an objective. One who has this gift is set in authority over others because he has earned the right to lead. He does this by serving those he leads in his example and character.

A leader will have followers not by demand or self-appointment, but by mutual recognition of others. Leaders will attract, model, and motivate people to be faithful, available, teachable, and reproducible. This type of leadership is acknowledged, not demanded.

This gift may be evidenced by observing the person that people turn to for help, those who carry existing leadership roles well, and those who are appointed leaders because of reputation. This gift may be exercised on the church board, in evangelism programs, Bible study groups, club programs, student ministries, or any other ministry.

12. The Gift of Administration (1 Corinthians 12:28)

The gift of administration involves efficient management and organization of resources and procedures. The person with this gift has the future planned and has plotted for all contingencies. This person loves to see things neat and in order; therefore his own life and manner is ordered and structured.

This gift may be seen in organizing events, overseeing communication, keeping records, arranging transportation, and ordering materials. It can also be seen in the administration of the church, whether it is in office and personnel management or in the effective administration of the church's education program. Everything is in its place when this person is in charge.

13. The Gift of Faith (1 Corinthians 12:9)

The gift of faith involves the extraordinary ability to believe God in the face of overwhelming obstacles. This is not saving faith, nor the faith all believers walk by in their daily lives. It is also not blind presumption whereby someone baptizes their own desires by claiming God wants something to come to pass. This gift allows one to believe without doubting that God's Word is true, no matter what the apparent outcome (James 1:6). Abraham displayed this kind of faith in Genesis 22. The gift of faith holds on when others give up, and it believes and sees things that others miss.

The leadership team of a church needs to have people gifted in faith who can see the possibilities for what God can do and begin to pray to bring it to pass. Such a person is also needed in counseling and in any planning group. This person works well with those gifted in leadership and exhortation.

Unity in Diversity

The lessons we learn from the fishing experiences of the first-century disciples help us to understand more about using our gifts. These fishermen couldn't have been successful if there were not those willing to pull on oars; others happy to mend their nets; others waiting on the shore to help pull in the nets; and still others with baskets and pots to carry and prepare the fish.

Similarly, a church works best when we work together *as a team*. We need preachers, musicians, ushers, custodians, servers, parking lot attendants, missionaries, and many others. Though believers have diverse gifts, they all work together for the com-mon good.

Someone once said, "A Christian's service involves each person of the Trinity." The gifts of the Spirit are the sovereign choice of the Holy Spirit; the place of our service is chosen by the

Son of God; and the actual working of our ministry is determined by the Father. This is made clear for us in 1 Corinthians 12:5-7:

> There are different kinds of service, but the same Lord [Jesus Christ]. There are different kinds of working, but the same God [the Father] works all of them in all men. Now to each one the manifestation of the Spirit [the Holy Spirit] is given for the common good.

If you watch the *In-Fisherman* television program, you will see a variety of hosts. Each member of Al Lindner's team has unique abilities. Some are experts in freshwater angling; others seem more relaxed in a saltwater environment. Ron Lindner is an expert on trolling the Great Lakes; Al seems to prefer the lighter rod challenges of smaller lakes and rivers. *God loves variety.* He loves to see diversity working in unity.

Don't worry about having a fully developed gift before you can serve. The only way your gift will become refined is to use it. So be faithful. Stay committed to the course. If you are faithful and obedient to God's Word, He will direct your ways and create opportunities for you to serve. You can connect with people who share your passion, vision, and interest. Your ministry should be a natural outgrowth of God's creative work in you.

Don't wait to be asked to get involved. Talk to your pastor, a friend, or another believer about your gifts and talents. Inquire about how you might use them to encourage others. There are plenty of single-parent kids who would love to have you share some time and teach them about your interests.

Every gift is important. The gifts that seem to receive more exposure are no more important than other gifts. Some of the most wonderful saints I know bake cookies and deliver them to people who visit their churches. Others prepare meals for the shut-ins and folks struggling with illness. One creative brother takes time off from work to join his pastor while he travels. He takes care of the driving, navigating, and logistical chores, thereby freeing the pastor to minister.

A Lesson from a Little Boy

The little boy who volunteered his lunch (five loaves of bread and two fish) to Jesus was using his gift (John 6:1-14). Jesus took his offerings and multiplied it for everyone's benefit. We can all learn something from this little boy's servant heart.

- God uses what you have to fill a need which you never could have filled.

- God uses you where you are to take you where you never could have gone.

- God uses what you can do to accomplish what you never could have done.

- God uses who you are to let you become who you never could have been.

The reason the In-Fisherman Network will continue to grow and prosper is because Al and Ron recognize the importance of not only using their gifts but of encouraging others in their giftedness. They look for every opportunity to support trusted staff members in exploring new horizons and dreams. What a wonderful example they set!

Discovering Your Spiritual Gift?

How can you discover your spiritual gift? I suggest you start off by praying. Then get involved in the work of ministry. Your gift(s) will surface in the midst of serving others. You might also ask your close friends what sort of giftedness they see in you. Go through a spiritual gift analysis like the one Pastor Jon McNeff developed. Read your Bible for insights. Go to a local Christian bookstore and pick up a good book on the subject. Discover your gifts and *use them to honor God*.

We are instructed in 1 Timothy 4:14 not to neglect our gifts. We are encouraged in 2 Timothy 1:6 to fan the flame of passion as we develop our gifts. We are commanded in

1 Corinthians 12:7 to do our part in service to Christ's beloved (the church) by using the spiritual gifts given to each of us.

Let none of us become so earthly minded that we fail to use the gifts that are designed for eternal value. Remember that the master who discovered that his servant had buried the one talent (silver coin) that was given to him was extremely displeased (*see* Matthew 25:14-30). But that same master rejoiced when his other servants revealed how they were able to double the talents given them. They had invested their talents and were rewarded with significant blessings. Those who had been willing to take risks, to make a commitment, and to put their gifts into service were by far the favored servants. How joyous a moment it must have been when their master declared his pleasure and his added blessings.

How are you using the gifts God has entrusted to you? Are you, like Al Lindner, making the most out of how God has blessed you?

Personal Growth

- How does Paul describe the variety of gifts that exist within the body (1 Corinthians 12)?

- Where do you see your spiritual gifts relative to the definitions provided in this passage?

- Unity in the body of Christ is a witness to the world. How can we work more effectively in coordinating our gifts (John 13:34-35; 17:23)?

PERSONAL PROFILE

Al Lindner

Background—Born in Chicago. Raised in Wisconsin.

Age When First Fish Caught—Five years old.

Favorite Bible Verse—Proverbs 16:3.

Family—Wife, Mary, two adult boys.

Favorite Fishing Hole—Lake of the Woods, Ontario, Canada.

Favorite Fishing Lure—Jig.

Preferred Equipment—Spinning.

Most Respected Fishing Pro or Instructor—Bill Binkelman, deceased publisher of *Fishing Facts*.

Personal Comments—"Hire the best people you can find, encourage their gifts, and let them go."

Understanding Fish Lingo

By their nature and makeup, fishermen are a unique breed. They have their own language and manner. Following are some of the basic terms used by those "who have heard the call of the fish."

angler—A person who pursues the sport of fishing with a rod, hook, and line as opposed to someone who uses dynamite or poison hemlock to capture his or her trophies.

bluegill—A sweet-tasting panfish sought mostly by ice fishermen who often suffer from the condition known as bluegills.

drag—A braking system on a reel that enables one to brake off fish with little effort. It also refers to having one's mother-in-law on a month-long backpack trip.

fishing guide—A local guy with a good knowledge of the water and a better knowledge of economics. He has managed to purchase a $28,000 river boat and $5,000 worth of tackle with the money of out-of-towners—all of whom were gullible enough to believe that by racing from one "secret spot" to another they could catch the trophy fish that has eluded the pros for years.

flying fish—What you see coming at you when you leave a mess of bluegill to be cleaned in your wife's kitchen sink.

hook—A highly irritating piece of metal usually found at the end of a line, on a plug, or in your thumb after plunging your hand into a jumbled tackle box.

keeper—Any fish larger than the lure or bait used to catch it.

quality time—Time spent relaxing on your boat with your kids, all the while telling them to keep quiet, knock off the clowning around, turn down the rap music, stay out of the livewell, and quit the worm racing.

rod—This is not a pole, unless you live below the Mason-Dixon line. Rods are used to fling or propel hooks, line, sinkers, bait, and/or lures in the general direction of a fish or a tree, whichever comes first.

snag—What an avid fisherman tells his buddies he's hit when his wife won't let him go fishing.

troll—A method of fishing that requires one to pull a lure behind a boat. It's also what one looks like upon returning home after a weeklong trip in the back country with the "good ol' boys."

trophy fish—Any fish weighing more than the gear used to catch it.

Bibliography

Arthur, Kay. *His Imprint, My Expression*. Eugene, OR: Harvest House Publishers, 1993.

_____. *Israel My Beloved*. Eugene, OR: Harvest House Publishers, 1996.

Barclay, William. *The Master's Men*. Nashville: Abingdon Press, 1959.

Black, Claudia. *Repeat After Me*. Denver: Mac Publishing, 1985.

Bright, Bill, et al. *Seven Promises of a Promise Keeper*. Colorado Springs: Focus on the Family Publishing, 1994.

Canfield, Jack and Mark Victor Hansen. *A 2nd Helping of Chicken Soup for the Soul*. Health Communications, Inc., 1995.

Carty, Jay. *Something's Fishy*. Portland, OR: Multnomah Press, 1960.

Crabb, Lawrence J. and Dan B. Allender. *Encouragment*. Grand Rapids, MI: Zondervan Publishing House, 1984.

Cunningham, Loren with Janice Rogers. *Is That Really You, God?* Seattle: YWAM Publishing, 1984.

Eisenman, Tom. *Temptations Men Face*. Downers Grove, IL: InterVarsity Press, 1990.

Finch, Raymond. *The Power of Prayer*. Boca Raton, FL: Globe Communications Corp., 1996.

Gilder, George. *Men and Marriage*. Gretna: Pelican Publishing Company, 1987.

Gurnsey, Dennis. *Thoroughly Married*. Waco, TX: Word Publishing, 1976.

Hansel, Tim. *Eating Problems for Breakfast*. Dallas: Word Publishing, 1988.

_____. *Through the Wilderness of Loneliness*. Elgin, IL: David C. Cook Publishing Co., 1991.

_____. *You Gotta Keep Dancin'*. Colorado Springs: Chariot Family Publishing, 1985.

Houston, Jimmy. *Caught Me a Big 'Un*. New York: Pocket Books, 1996.

Hybels, Bill and Mark Mittelberg. *Becoming a Contagious Christian*. Grand Rapids, MI: Zondervan Publishing House, 1994.

Johnson, Dave. *Path to Victory: A Sports New Testament*. Colorado Springs: International Bible Society, 1984.

Kaniut, Larru. *Alaska Bear Tales*. Anchorage: Alaska Northwest Publishing Co., 1983.

Lundstrom, Lowell. *Daily Power Thoughts for Busy People*. Sisseton, SD: Lowell Lundstrom Ministries, Inc., 1983.

MacDonald, Gordon. *The Effective Father*. Wheaton, IL: Tyndale House Publishers, 1981.

Maclean, Norman. *A River Runs Through It*. Chicago: The University of Chicago Press, 1976.

McManus, Patrick F. *Never Sniff a Gift Fish*. New York: Holt, Rinehart and Winston, 1979.

McVey, Steve. *Grace Walk*. Eugene, OR: Harvest House Publishers, 1995.

Minirth, Frank and Mary, et al. *Passages of Marriage*. Nashville: Thomas Nelson Publishers, 1991.

Ogilvie, Lloyd John. *Four Steps to Living Fearless and Free*. Waco, TX: Word Publishing, 1987.

Reece, Maynard. *Fish and Fishing*. Des Moines: Meredith Press, 1963.

Rhodes, Ron. *Angels Among Us*. Eugene, OR: Harvest House Publishers, 1995.

_____. *The Heart of Christianity*. Eugene, OR: Harvest House Publishers, 1996.

Scazzero, Peter. *Old Testament Characters*. Downers Grove, IL: InterVarsity Press, 1988.

Smalley, Gary and John Trent. *The Blessing*. Nashville: Thomas Nelson Publishers, 1979.

Stanley, Charles. *How to Handle Adversity*. Nashville: Thomas Nelson Publishers, 1989.

Stinnett, Nick and John DeFrain. *Secrets of Strong Families*. New York: Berkley Books, 1985.

Swindoll, Charles. *Hand Me Another Brick*. Nashville: Thomas Nelson Publishers, 1978.

_____. *Intimacy with the Almighty*. Dallas: Word Publishing, 1996.

_____. *Living Above the Level of Mediocrity*. Waco, TX: Word Publishing, 1987.

_____. *Strengthening Your Grip*. Waco, TX: Word Publishing, 1982.

_____. *The Quest for Character*. Portland, OR: Multnomah Press, 1987.

_____. *Three Steps Forward, Two Steps Back*. Nashville: Thomas Nelson Press, 1980.

Wright, H. Norman. *Quiet Moments for Couples*. Eugene, OR: Harvest House Publishers, 1995.

Notes

Chapter 2—The Christian Disciple

1. Jay Carty, *Something's Fishy* (Portland, OR: Multnomah, 1990), pp. 11-16.
2. Ron Rhodes, *The Heart of Christianity* (Eugene, OR: Harvest House Publishers, 1996), pp. 85-86.
3. Jim Grassi, *Promising Waters* (Eugene, OR: Harvest House Publishers, 1996), p. 18.
4. Carty, *Something's Fishy*, p. 74.

Chapter 3—The Obedient Disciple

1. Charles Stanley, message delivered in Atlanta, Georgia, 1992.
2. Raymond Finch, *The Power of Prayer* (Boca Raton, FL: Globe Communications Corp., 1996), p. 4.

Chapter 4—The Determined Disciple

1. Mark Hoff, *Fishing—An Angler's Miscellany* (Kansas City, MO: Andrews and McMeel, 1995), p. 34.
2. James Robison, *Thank God, I'm Free* (Nashville, TN: Thomas Nelson Publishers, 1988), pp. 19-20.
3. Ibid., pp. 26-27.
4. James Robison, *Knowing God As Father* (Fort Worth, TX: Life Today, 1996), pp. 14-15.
5. Ibid., pp. 22-23.
6. Robison, *Thank God, I'm Free*, p. 60.
7. Ibid., p. 63
8. Ibid., p. 72
9. Ibid., p. 98
10. Ibid., p. 90

Chapter 5—Living Under Grace

1. Steve McVey, *Grace Walk* (Eugene, OR: Harvest House Publishers, 1995), p. 172.
2. Charles Swindoll, *The Grace Awakening* (Dallas, TX: Word Publishing, 1990), p. 9.
3. Carroll E. Simox, *3,000 Quotations on Christian Themes* (Grand Rapids, MI: Baker Book House, 1975), p. 134.

4. Donald Grey Barnhouse, *Romans: Man's Ruin*, vol. 1 (Grand Rapids, MI: Wm. B. Eerdmans Publishing Company, 1952), p. 72.
5. Swindoll, *Grace Awakening*, ch. 11.
6. *The Hymnal for Worship and Celebration* (Waco, TX: Word Music, 1986), #202.

Chapter 6—Living by Faith

1. Ed Hindson, *Men of the Promise* (Eugene, OR: Harvest House Publishers, 1996), p. 16.
2. Loren Cunningham, *Is That Really You, God?* (Seattle, WA: YWAM Publishing, 1984), pp. 148-51.

Chapter 7—Living Without Anxiety

1. Lloyd John Ogilvie, *Four Steps to Living Fearless and Free* (Waco, TX: Word Publishing, 1987).
2. Ibid.

Chapter 8—Joy-Filled Living

1. Mother Teresa (b. 1910), Albanian-born Roman Catholic missionary, *A Gift for God*, "Joy" (1975).
2. Tim Hansel, *You Gotta Keep Dancin'* (Elgin, IL: David C. Cook, 1985), p. 15.
3. Ibid., p. 47.
4. Ibid., p. 55.

Chapter 9—Conquering Temptation

1. Jimmy Houston, *Caught Me a Big 'Un . . .* (New York, NY: Pocket Books, 1996), pp. 3-4.
2. Kay Arthur, *His Imprint My Expression* (Eugene, OR: Harvest House Publishers, 1993), pp. 120-28.
3. George Gilder, *Men and Marriage* (Gretna: Pelican Publishing Company, 1987), ch. 1.
4. Tom L. Eisenman, *Temptations Men Face* (Downers Grove, IL: InterVarsity Press, 1990), p. 54.
5. Cherly Forbes, as quoted in Eisenman, *Temptations*, p. 109.

Chapter 10—Walking in Integrity

1. Charles Swindoll, message delivered at Evangelical Free Church, Fullerton, CA, July 24, 1988.

Chapter 11—The Courageous Heart

1. Tim Hanzel, *Through the Wilderness of Loneliness* (Elgin, IL: David C. Cook Publishing Co., 1991).
2. *San Francisco Chronicle*, Sporting Green, p. B1.
3. E.C. McKenzie, *14,000 Quips and Quotes* (Grand Rapids, MI: Baker Book House, 1990), p. 114.

4. Lawrence O. Richards, *The 365-Day Devotional Commentary* (Wheaton, IL: Victor Books, 1987), p. 185.

5. Carrol E. Simcox, *3000 Quotations on Christian Themes* (Grand Rapids, MI: Baker Book House, 1975), p. 162.

Chapter 12—Perilous Pride

1. Charles Swindoll, *Old Testament Characters—Bible Study Guide* (Fullerton, CA: Insights for Living, 1973), pp. 62-67.

2. Carroll E. Simcox, *3000 Quotations on Christian Themes* (Grand Rapids, MI: Baker Book House, 1988), p. 102.

Chapter 13—The Healthy Christian Family

1. Gary Bauer, *The Family: Preserving America's Future* (Washington, DC: The United States Department of Interior).

2. Gordon MacDonald, *The Effective Father* (Wheaton, IL: Tyndale House Publishers), pp. 79-80.

Chapter 14—To Love and to Honor

1. Nick Lyons, *Fishing Widows* (New York, NY: Crown Publishers, Inc., 1974), pp. 17-18.

2. Thomas Kinkade, *Simpler Times* (Eugene, OR: Harvest House Publishers, 1996), p. 11.

3. H. Norman Wright, *Quiet Moments for Couples* (Eugene, OR: Harvest House Publishers, 1995).

Chapter 15—Encouraging Others

1. E.C. McKenzie, *14,000 Quips and Quotes* (Grand Rapids, MI: Baker Books, 1990), p. 155.

2. Lawrence J. Crabb, Jr. and Dan B. Allender, *Encouragement* (Grand Rapids, MI: Zondervan Publishing House, 1984), p. 25.

3. Gary Smalley and John Trent, *The Blessing* (Nashville, TN: Thomas Nelson, 1979), p. 82.

Chapter 16—Discovering and Using Your Spiritual Gifts

1. Jon McNeff, *Power Tools: Spiritual Gift Inventory* (Walnut Creek, CA: Evangelical Free Church of Walnut Creek Press, 1996), p. 2.

2. Ibid., pp. 13-16. If you would like to order McNeff's *Power Talks: Spiritual Gift Inventory*, write to the Evangelical Free Church of Walnut Creek, 2303 Ygnacio Valley Road, Walnut Creek, CA, 94598. Send $5.00.

3. Charles Swindoll, message delivered at Evangelical Free Church, Fullerton, CA, June 23, 1991.

A Personal Message

1. Norman Maclean, *A River Runs Through It* (Chicago, IL: The University of Chicago Press, 1976), p. 1.

A Personal Message

Dear friend,

As you've seen in this book, there is a unique connection between fishing and Christian discipleship. So many of Christ's teachings involved correlations and parables from fishing experiences.

The connection is so obvious that even Hollywood has capitalized on the relationship. The movie *A River Runs Through It* called this nation back to an appreciation for fishing. The words of the narrator still ring in my ears:

> In our family, there was no clear line between religion and fly-fishing. We lived at the junction of great trout rivers in Western Montana, and our father was a Presbyterian minister and a fly fisherman who tied his own flies and taught others. He told us about Christ's disciples being fishermen, and we were left to assume, as my brother and I did, that all first-class fishermen of the Sea of Galilee were fly fishermen and that John, the favorite, was a dry-fly fisherman.[1]

Let's Go Fishing Ministries (LGFM) has been telling people about this unique connection for over 17 years. The purpose of LGFM is to help train disciples while strengthening America's families through a variety of outdoor programs. We provide church outreach activities, men's fellowship opportunities, "Special Kids Days" for the disabled, ministry to single-parent families, and conference center presentations.

If you would like to receive our free quarterly newsletter or learn more about Let's Go Fishing Ministries, I invite you to write:

Jim Grassi
Let's Go Fishing Ministries
P.O. Box 434
Moraga, CA 94556

I pray that the principles in this book will inspire you to be a disciple of the Master Fisherman—Jesus Christ. Keep on fishing for Jesus!

In His service,
Jim Grassi

Other Good
Harvest House Reading

PROMISING WATERS
by *Jim Grassi*

Filled to the limit with anecdotes, humor, and adventure stories, *Promising Waters* will catch the attention of every man, outdoorsman or not, who wants to know more about walking with Jesus every day. International fishing coach Jim Grassi explores the parallels between fishing and discipleship, showing men how to create an atmosphere of openness, wisdom, and guidance that promotes deep relationships.

15 MINUTES ALONE WITH GOD FOR MEN
by *Bob Barnes*

A devotional that encourages men to fulfill their high calling as husbands, fathers, workers, and companions. Explores the vast riches and depths of God for men wanting to walk with Him, and not just talk about Him.

THE INTIMATE HUSBAND
by *Richard Furman*

The account of one man's decision to regain the love of his wife and save his faltering marriage. Talking with successful husbands around the country, Furman found the tools to restablish the intimacy God intended.

MEN OF THE PROMISE
by *Ed Hindson*

Discover the refreshingly simple and fulfilling calling God designed especially for men. Hindson's inspirational study of Old Testament figures encourages men to discover the many ways God wants to use them today. Excellent for groups.

THE TOTAL CHRISTIAN GUY
by *Phil Callaway*

Venture into the mind of a Christian guy. Find out why he would rather pray than move furniture. Uncover his mysterious fascination with remote controls. In this collection of humorous stories, you'll meet guys like Phil—guys who fall, but can get back up, who can laugh in the face of the storm.

Dear Reader,

We would appreciate hearing from you regarding this Harvest House nonfiction book. It will enable us to continue to give you the best in Christian publishing.

1. What most influenced you to purchase *Heaven on Earth?*
   - ❑ Author
   - ❑ Subject matter
   - ❑ Backcover copy
   - ❑ Recommendations
   - ❑ Cover/Title
   - ❑ Other_____

2. Where did you purchase this book?
   - ❑ Christian bookstore
   - ❑ General bookstore
   - ❑ Department store
   - ❑ Grocery store
   - ❑ Other_____

3. Your overall rating of this book?
   - ❑ Excellent ❑ Very good ❑ Good ❑ Fair ❑ Poor

4. How likely would you be to purchase other books by this author?
   - ❑ Very likely ❑ Not very likely ❑ Somewhat likely ❑ Not at all

5. What types of books most interest you? (Check all that apply.)
   - ❑ Men's Books
   - ❑ Marriage Books
   - ❑ Current Issues
   - ❑ Self Help/Psychology
   - ❑ Bible Studies
   - ❑ Fiction
   - ❑ Biographies
   - ❑ Children's Books
   - ❑ Youth Books
   - ❑ Other_____

6. Please check the box next to your age group.
   - ❑ Under 18 ❑ 18-24 ❑ 25-34 ❑ 35-44 ❑ 45-54 ❑ 55 and over

Mail to: Editorial Director
Harvest House Publishers
1075 Arrowsmith
Eugene, OR 97402

Name _____

Address _____

State _____ Zip _____

Thank you for helping us to help you in future publications!